THE SMARTEST PORTFOLIO YOU'LL EVER OWN

Also by Daniel R. Solin

DOES YOUR BROKER OWE YOU MONEY?

THE SMARTEST INVESTMENT BOOK YOU'LL EVER READ

THE SMARTEST 401(K) BOOK YOU'LL EVER READ

THE SMARTEST RETIREMENT BOOK YOU'LL EVER READ

THE SMARTEST PORTFOLIO YOU'LL EVER OWN

A Do-It-Yourself Breakthrough Strategy

Daniel R. Solin

A PERIGEE BOOK

A PERIGEE BOOK
Published by the Penguin Group
Penguin Group (USA) Inc.
375 Hudson Street, New York, New York 10014, USA
Penguin Group (Canada), 90 Eglinton Avenue East, Suite 700, Toronto, Ontario M4P 2Y3, Canada
(a division of Pearson Penguin Canada Inc.)
Penguin Books Ltd., 80 Strand, London WC2R 0RL, England
Penguin Group Ireland, 25 St. Stephen's Green, Dublin 2, Ireland (a division of Penguin Books Ltd.)
Penguin Group (Australia), 250 Camberwell Road, Camberwell, Victoria 3124, Australia
(a division of Pearson Australia Group Pty. Ltd.)
Penguin Books India Pvt. Ltd., 11 Community Centre, Panchsheel Park, New Delhi—110 017, India
Penguin Group (NZ), 67 Apollo Drive, Rosedale, Auckland 0632, New Zealand
(a division of Pearson New Zealand Ltd.)
Penguin Books (South Africa) (Pty.) Ltd., 24 Sturdee Avenue, Rosebank, Johannesburg 2196,
South Africa

Penguin Books Ltd., Registered Offices: 80 Strand, London WC2R 0RL, England

While the author has made every effort to provide accurate telephone numbers and Internet addresses at the time of publication, neither the publisher nor the author assumes any responsibility for errors or for changes that occur after publication. Further, the publisher does not have any control over and does not assume any responsibility for author or third-party websites or their content.

First edition: September 2011

Library of Congress Cataloging-in-Publication Data

Solin, Daniel R.
    The smartest portfolio you'll ever own : a do-it-yourself breakthrough strategy / Daniel R. Solin.—
1st ed.
        p.   cm.
    Includes index.
    ISBN 978-0-399-53706-6
    1. Portfolio management.   2. Investments.   I. Title.
    HG4529.5.S66 2011
    332.6—dc23   2011017944

PRINTED IN THE UNITED STATES OF AMERICA

10 9 8 7 6 5 4 3 2 1

PUBLISHER'S NOTE: This publication is designed to provide accurate and authoritative information in regard to the subject matter covered. It is sold with the understanding that the publisher is not engaged in rendering legal, accounting, or other professional services. If you require legal advice or other expert assistance, you should seek the services of a competent professional. Continued on page 197.

Most Perigee books are available at special quantity discounts for bulk purchases for sales promotions, premiums, fund-raising, or educational use. Special books, or book excerpts, can also be created to fit specific needs. For details, write: Special Markets, Penguin Group (USA) Inc., 375 Hudson Street, New York, New York 10014.

To Patricia, for whom kindness and compassion are a way of life.

CONTENTS

PART THREE
The Smartest Portfolios

PART FOUR
Smartest Alternative Portfolios

PART FIVE
Going It Alone or Getting Advice

INTRODUCTION

A Lesson from Einstein

Everything should be made as simple as possible, but not simpler.

—Albert Einstein

We can learn a lot about investing from Albert Einstein. As legend has it, when he died, he met two men and a woman outside the pearly gates. Always one to strike up a conversation, he asked them about their IQs.

The woman said her IQ was 190. Einstein was excited. He said, "We can discuss my theory of relativity."

The first man said his IQ was 150. "Good," said Einstein. "We can discuss global warming and arms reduction."

The second man sheepishly said, "I'm sorry, but my IQ is only 100. I'm afraid I won't have anything to discuss with you."

Unfazed, Einstein looked at him intently and said, "That's not a problem at all. Where do you think the market is headed?"

Here's the real skinny on investing:

- It's not complicated.

- No one has a clue where the markets are headed—not even Albert Einstein!

- Holding individual stocks or bonds exposes you to higher risk without higher expected return.

- Holding any actively managed mutual fund increases your costs and reduces your expected return.

- Using the services of brokers or advisers who claim to be able to beat the markets significantly reduces your chances of capturing market returns.

- The free market system works. Stock prices are random and efficient. There is no mispricing.

- There's a wealth of irrefutable data supporting these views.

The idea that index based investing is simple and vastly superior to stock picking, market timing, and efforts to pick the next "hot" mutual fund manager shakes the very foundation of the securities industry. If investing were so simple, why would you need their services? Why should you purchase their actively managed mutual funds and annuities? Why should you listen to their stock picking and market timing recommendations?

The value of do-it-yourself investing in index funds was the basic message of my previous book, *The Smartest Investment Book You'll Ever Read*. If you followed the recommendations in that book, you emerged from the market crash of 2008 largely unscathed because you were in a portfolio appropriate for your risk tolerance. When the markets tanked, your paper losses were tolerable. You did not panic. You held on, and benefited from the rapid recovery in 2009–2011.

The success of *The Smartest Investment Book* spawned tens of thousands of savvy investors. They wanted to know if there was any way to improve the returns of the index fund portfolios I recommended.

The answer is yes. These portfolios are well known to a small group of advisers who understand the data and have access to the funds (available only through them) necessary to construct a portfolio that could achieve this goal. Until now, if you were an investor who wanted to go it alone, you did not have access to the funds, or the knowledge, to truly maximize your returns. Now you will.

A note of caution and full disclosure: I am an adviser. I recommend passively managed, risk-adjusted portfolios to my clients, following the principles used to construct the SuperSmart Portfolio set forth in this book. I believe most investors are well served by retaining an adviser who understands and implements the sound, academic underpinnings of these portfolios.

But I have to be realistic. I know many of you will continue to use brokers or advisers who claim to be able to beat the markets by picking stocks or recommending hot mutual fund managers. What you will learn in this book will give you the ammunition you need to protect yourself from these "investment professionals."

I also know many of you may not have a portfolio large enough to interest advisers who follow the sound investing principles I describe in this book. Or you may simply want to do it yourself and save the advisory fees, even when confronted with facts showing that paying the fee is in your best interest, when you consider total returns.

For whatever reason, I believe you should be empowered to have the most optimal portfolio available. I wrote this book so you can do just that. The rest is up to you.

If you come across a word or phrase you don't understand, please refer to the Glossary. You will most likely find it there.

Finally, most investors will benefit from a discussion of what they are currently doing wrong and a review of the academic underpinnings for the Smartest Portfolios. For those who just can't wait to see the allocations and funds in the SuperSmart Portfolio, you will find this information in Chapter 21. Comparable information for the three alternative Smartest Portfolios can be found in Chapters 23 through 25.

PART ONE

The Wrong Way

If you are like 90% of investors, you're investing the wrong way. You abandon common sense and basic principles of due diligence when it comes to managing your money. An entire industry makes a living fostering bad investor behavior. Their conduct enriches them. It's depriving you of superior market returns, which are easily attainable.

Before you can invest the right way, you need to understand what you are doing wrong.

CHAPTER 1

A Battle for Your Brain

Shaped a little like a loaf of French country bread, our brain is a crowded chemistry lab, bustling with nonstop neural conversations.
—Diane Ackerman, *The Alchemy of Mind*

I am going to tell you exactly how to invest your hard-earned money to maximize your returns and minimize risk. I will not just spout abstract theory. I will give you the tools to determine which portfolio is right for you. I will tell you exactly which funds you should invest in. You can implement my recommendations in a couple of hours, at most.

My recommendations don't reflect just my opinion. They are the product of the finest minds in finance today, backed by reams of academic studies. Most people who don't agree with them are not familiar with the data or have a vested interest in leading you down the wrong financial path (like "market-beating" brokers and advisers).

Is there a catch or a hidden agenda? Is this too good to be true?

Absolutely not.

For those who want to go it alone, I give you the tools to do so. Just set up an account with an online broker, place the trades for the group of funds you have selected from the options I provide to you, and you are on the way to a demonstrably superior way to invest. The online brokerage firm will profit, but their costs per trade are very low. Many offer to place trades for $7 or less.

The funds I recommend do charge management fees, but their expenses (known as *expense ratios*) are as low as 0.07% per year. I don't benefit. I have no interest in the brokerage firms or in any of the recommended funds.

So, what's the rub?

Your brain.

Studies of neuroeconomics, an interdisciplinary field that seeks to explain human decision making, show that emotions drive investment decisions as much (or more) than objective data.

Powerful emotions, most notably greed and fear, are very dangerous because most of us are not aware of their potent influence as they activate chemical secretions in the brain. The possibility of a "big score" in the markets actually releases dopamine in the brain. Brain images of investors as they watch a stock that is rapidly increasing in value are remarkably similar to scans of those addicted to drugs or alcohol.

According to Jason Zweig, author of *Your Money and Your Brain*, it's the dopamine rush that explains "why we play lotto, invest in IPOs [initial public offerings of stocks], keep too much money in too few stocks and invest with active portfolio managers instead of index funds."

Other behavior factors also influence our investment decisions and keep us from adopting simple strategies that would benefit us financially.

A well-known basis for misperceptions called the *halo effect* was first documented in 1920 by E. L. Thorndike. The halo effect refers to the tendency to form an overall opinion about a person or circumstance based on a perception in one area. If, for example, we find one trait we like about a person, we carry that positive evaluation over to other traits. In one study, subjects were shown one of two videos with the same talk by the same lecturer. In one video the lecturer was in "nice guy" mode. In another, he was "nasty." Those who viewed the nice guy video thought of the lecturer as more attractive than those who viewed the nasty video.

The Madoff Ponzi scheme is the poster child for how the halo effect can affect investors. The perception of "Bernie" (which sounds almost cuddly) was that he was highly reputable, a pillar of integrity, and totally trustworthy. These perceptions of his personality and his background (including a stint as chairman of NASDAQ) caused investors to slide down a slippery slope. They assumed the investments in his fund were as reputable as he appeared to be and failed to do basic due diligence, ignoring obvious red flags. There was a subconscious carryover of what they believed were positive personal traits to an investment that they should have evaluated independently.

Another study showed that mutual funds that changed their names to take advantage of current hot investment styles significantly increased inflows of assets, despite no increase in performance.

The ramifications of neuroeconomics are profound.

First, understand that your brain may be pushing you toward the thrill of short-term decisions, when your real focus should be on long-term ones.

Second, stockbrokers understand the power of neuroeconomics much better than you do. They use the halo effect and other emotions (primarily greed and fear) to drive you to take action that is good for them and bad for you.

Remember what happened during the 2008 market crash? The financial media went into overdrive, positing all kinds of scenarios of financial Armageddon. Investors were encouraged by their brokers to flee to safety. Many followed this flawed advice, selling stocks and buying bonds, gold, and money market funds. This was great for brokerage firms. Commission income surged.

How did listening to this advice work out for you? If you had done nothing, you would have recovered all (or most) of your losses when the markets surged back from 2009 to 2011.

This is really a battle over your brain. I want your brain to dispassionately assess the data and information I am giving you. Your stockbroker wants to trigger a chemical reaction in your brain that will cause you to abandon common sense and act emotionally.

What's the Point?

Understanding how your brain can interfere with making intelligent investment decisions can lead you to make smarter decisions that will help you reach your financial goals.

CHAPTER 2

In Bizarro World, These Traits Would Be Valued

Yeah. Like Bizarro Superman. Superman's exact opposite, who lives in
the backwards bizarro world. Up is down, down is up. He says "hello"
when he leaves, "good-bye" when he arrives.

—Jerry Seinfeld

Almost everything about the behavior of investors is mystifying. You work so hard for your money. You are meticulous, diligent, and cautious. No one is going to take advantage of you or your company on your watch!

You carefully reference-check the backgrounds of new employees. You even pay for an extensive criminal search and verify college transcripts. You do the same with vendors. Lack of honesty or integrity, even on a small scale, is a deal breaker.

How do you apply these traits when it comes to investing those hard-earned dollars? Many of you continue to use brokers employed by brokerage firms with a long history of acting against the best interest of their clients.

In 1990, we had the junk bond scandal, culminating in a guilty plea by junk bond king Michael Milken to multiple felony charges and an agreement to pay penalties of $600 million. Milken ran the high-yield bond department at Drexel Burnham Lambert. Other prominent traders caught up in the scandal included Ivan Boesky, who pleaded guilty to securities fraud as a part of a larger insider trading investigation.

In April 2003, 10 of the largest brokerage firms agreed to pay $1.4 billion to settle charges their research had misled investors. The allegation was that the firms basically sold out their retail clients (that's you!) to curry favor with the companies for whom they did lucrative underwriting business.

Some of the internal documents obtained by the Securities and Exchange Commission (SEC) were chilling. In one famous email, Jack Grubman, who had obtained near-deity status as the telecommunications analyst for the firm known at that time as Salomon Smith Barney, called a company he was recommending to retail clients of the firm a "pig." Emails from other analysts referred to highly touted companies in even more unflattering terms.

The settling firms were a who's-who of the securities industry and included Credit Suisse, Merrill Lynch, Lehman Brothers, Morgan Stanley, J.P. Morgan, and Goldman Sachs.

In April 2004, Janus Capital Group agreed to pay $100 million in fines to resolve charges it allowed favored clients to engage in excessive trading in its mutual funds that hurt other investors. Putnam Investments and Bank of America had previously agreed to settlements involving similar conduct.

In March 2006, the SEC announced a settlement with Bear Stearns involving allegations it engaged in "late trading" and "deceptive market timing." Bear Stearns agreed to a penalty of $250 million.

In 2007, Bank of America agreed to pay $26 million to settle allegations its traders used information generated by its analysts to trade stock before the information was disseminated to the public. You would think the April 2003 $1.4 billion settlement of the analyst scandal involving similar practices would have had a long-lasting effect.

Not so. According to the SEC, the analysts also issued false research, touting companies in an effort to secure their underwriting business. Sound familiar?

There were a litany of other enforcement actions against other members of the securities industry, but I'm sure you get the point. (For a timeline of various proceedings against members of the securities industry, check out http://timelinesdb.com/listevents.php?subjid=575& title=SEC.)

All this pales in comparison to the conduct that contributed to the 2008 market crash. This debacle, in which toxic subprime mortgages were sold to clueless buyers with low credit ratings, almost precipitated a global depression. Who were the main players in this mess? The biggest ones were Bank of America/Merrill Lynch, UBS, J.P. Morgan Chase, Citigroup, Morgan Stanley, Wells Fargo, Royal Bank of Scotland, Credit Suisse, Goldman Sachs, and Barclays.

Some of the revelations about the inner workings of these firms as this crisis unfolded are revealing and disgusting. According to one report, "The 'Subsidy'" by Jake Bernstein and Jesse Eisinger (*ProPublica*), several years before the crisis gathered full steam, traders at Merrill Lynch refused to buy the supposedly safe portions of the mortgage-backed securities Merrill was creating. The traders obviously knew what the public was about to learn: These securities were toxic.

Merrill is reported to have solved this problem by forming a new group to take on the money-losing securities. By paying millions of dollars of bonuses to the traders in this group, the money machine continued for Merrill, until the house of cards collapsed, causing losses of hundreds of billions of dollars to clueless individual investors.

Senator Carl Levin, the chairman of the Permanent Subcommittee of Investigations, issued a scathing 640-page report on the conduct of Goldman Sachs. The report found that Goldman Sachs profited from the decline in mortgage-related securities at the same time as it was peddling these "investments" to its clients. The fallout from this chicanery was immense. Merrill Lynch was sold to Bank of America. The venerable Lehman Brothers filed for bankruptcy. American International Group suffered massive losses and needed a $40 billion lifeline from the Federal Reserve to stay in business. The cash infusion subsequently shot up to $150 billion.

Bear Stearns was sold for peanuts to J.P. Morgan Chase, in a deal backed by the taxpayers—you and me. Goldman Sachs and Morgan Stanley Smith Barney converted to commercial banks.

The crisis was exacerbated by blatant conflicts of interest at the credit-rating agencies, whose ratings misled buyers into believing that snake oil (risky subprime mortgages) was really vitamin water (AAA-rated bonds). The SEC subsequently approved measures to strengthen oversight of credit-rating agencies. In the understatement of the century, the SEC announced findings of "serious deficiencies" with the process. Those of us who live in the real world do not need a study to help us understand the existence of a conflict of interest when the people doing the credit rating at the credit-rating agencies are paid by the issuers of the securities being rated.

The scandals involving big Wall Street players continue unabated and undeterred. On December 7, 2010, Bank of America agreed to pay $137 million to settle charges it defrauded buyers of municipal bond derivatives.

It's not just the extent of the fraudulent conduct of the securities industry that's so striking. It's the fact that it involves the largest and best-known players.

The conclusion is inescapable. This is an industry infected by systemic greed and the absence of an ethical or moral code of conduct. They want your money. They will do or say anything to get it. They view the fines they pay as simply a cost of doing business.

All this, standing alone, is reason enough for you to refuse to do business with them. Unfortunately, there's more. The entire premise of the way they manage your money is fatally flawed, rife with conflict of interest, and designed to transfer your money to them.

You don't live in bizarro world. Walk into your broker's office and say good-bye. He or she will understand it doesn't mean "hello."

What's the Point?

These dogs have had more than their one free bite.
Don't give them another.

CHAPTER 3

Investing Without Eddie O'Neal

The nature of any human being, certainly anyone on Wall Street, is "the better deal you give the customer, the worse deal it is for you."
—Bernie Madoff

osing money is always bad. Losing it to a crook is even worse.

In 2006, I was the cofounder and a principal in an investment advisory firm. My partner in this venture was Eddie O'Neal, then an assistant professor of finance at the Babcock Graduate School of Management at Wake Forest University. At the time, hedge funds were all the rage and we were under pressure from our clients to generate the kind of outsized returns these funds were reporting.

In the latter part of 2006, Eddie and I traveled to New York to meet with a senior executive of the Fairfield Sentry Fund. The executive explained that his firm had almost $20 billion in assets under management, of which approximately $6 billion were invested with an advisory firm run by Bernie Madoff. He reviewed Madoff's stellar returns with us. They were impressive—a remarkably consistent 1% a month, regardless of market conditions, with very few exceptions.

Our man from Fairfield thought there was a possibility he could use the leverage of his firm to get our clients in on the action—if we invested through Fairfield—even though (according to him) the current demand exceeded Madoff's ability to manage more money.

Eddie, who's as smart as he is self-effacing, sat quietly throughout the meeting. Just as we were about to leave, he asked one question: "How do you monitor Madoff's performance?" It was obviously a question the Fairfield executive had answered many times before. In a mildly condescending tone, he told us they had "the most sophisticated monitoring possible" located on-site at Madoff's offices. He stated that "when a keystroke is placed by a Madoff trader, it records at our offices." The marvels of technology! I was impressed.

As we left and got into a cab, I turned to Eddie and asked him what he thought. He looked at me and said, "I don't believe the returns." I asked him what due diligence he would have to do to alleviate his concerns. He said, "None, because these returns are not possible." That was it. We never pursued discussions with Fairfield or with any other hedge fund.

Many others were suspicious of Madoff's operations long before December 2008, when he confessed to running a massive Ponzi scheme. Spanish banking Goliath Banco Santander invested $3.2 billion of its clients' assets with Madoff. According to an internal report, its staff knew that his operations were "shrouded in secrecy" and lacked independent verification.

You didn't need Eddie's historical perspective on market returns to question Madoff's operations. It would not have been difficult for anyone to spot the biggest red flags. He had no independent custodian for the assets of his clients. His accounting firm was not exactly one of the Big Four. The three-person firm that certified Madoff's books had previously advised the American Institute of Certified Public Accountants that it didn't conduct audits! The firm had only one active accountant, and he operated from a small office in a strip mall.

So how did the most sophisticated feeder funds get duped by this primitive scheme? The list includes not only the Fairfield Greenwich

Group but other investment giants like Banco Santander, Tremont Group Holdings, Kingate, Mount Capital, and Access International Advisors Europe, whose cofounder committed suicide after Madoff's scheme was exposed.

Why? Just follow the money and the answer is obvious: fees. By some accounts, total fees generated by feeder funds from clients who invested with Madoff amounted to an unbelievable $790 million over the years! Fairfield Sentry is reported to have earned more than $500 million in fees since 2003 from funds it invested with Madoff.

These firms had the ability to detect this primitive fraud. They turned a blind eye to it and sold out their clients for the obscene fees they were earning by simply endorsing their clients' checks over to Madoff.

You don't need Eddie O'Neal to assist you with your investment decisions. But you should know better than to deal with people who have consistently sacrificed your well-being to fatten their own (already bulging) wallets.

What's the Point?

The securities industry is a wolf in sheep's clothing.

CHAPTER 4

Join a Wise Crowd

What distinguishes index funds is that they don't presume to have greater wisdom than the collective market, but instead try to channel its wisdom to your advantage.

—Zack O'Malley Greenburg, financial journalist

am frequently invited to talk to investment clubs. I have a standard response: You don't want me because I will tell you either to disband your group or to call it a social club because that's what it is.

More often than not, they persist. They want to *prove* to me that I am wrong. They believe they can demonstrate how they can beat the markets.

Members of investment clubs believe they benefit from the collective wisdom of the group. We have common ground on this issue. We both believe there is something to be learned from the wisdom of crowds, but diverge sharply on the conclusions to be drawn from it.

It's well documented that the collective wisdom of very large groups of people results in decisions that are often superior to those made by any individual member of the group.

In his excellent book *The Wisdom of Crowds: Why the Many Are Smarter Than the Few and How Collective Wisdom Shapes Business, Economies, Societies and Nations*, James Surowiecki gives many examples of collective wisdom. Here's one: The average guesses by a crowd at a country fair of the weight of an ox were more accurate than most of the individual estimates. That average was also closer to the actual weight than the estimates of cattle experts.

Surowiecki notes that not all crowds are wise, particularly those characterized by homogeneity and those subject to emotional factors (like peer pressure) and imitation (where initial decisions by group leaders are copied by others). A wise crowd is one that features a broad diversity of opinion and independence, among other traits.

Investment clubs have the traits of an unwise crowd. They typically lack diversity and have a tendency to be influenced by opinions of other members of the club. Their collective judgment about stock prices is likely to be "unwise" and certainly not as valuable as the views of the totality of the investment community outside their group.

The data on investment club performance support this view. One exhaustive study by Brad M. Barber and Terrance Odean showed that 60% of clubs underperformed the market. The average club underperformed a broad market index by 3% a year. Viewed through the lens of the wisdom of crowds, this makes perfect sense.

Club members fight tenaciously to justify their validity. I recently addressed a club consisting of a group of wealthy individuals at a gated community in Naples, Florida. They told me the past returns of the Vanguard Wellington Fund (VWELX) "proved" they could beat the market and challenged me to persuade them otherwise. They picked an excellent fund to underpin their argument. The Wellington Fund is a balanced fund, with a low expense ratio (the operating costs of the fund) of 0.34%. Its annualized return for the 10 years ending September 30, 2000, was 14.12%. For the ensuing 10-year period, its return was 5.58%. These returns exceeded the median returns for all balanced funds by 0.71% in the first 10 years and by 3.18% in the second. They put this question to me: Given the stellar performance of this fund, why did I believe it was unlikely their group could not beat the market?

I looked at the performance of all 60 balanced funds for which data were available for both 10-year periods. Here's what I found: When funds outperformed in one period, they rarely were able to repeat that outperformance in the following period. The data demonstrated a statistically meaningless correlation between stellar performance in one period and similar performance in the next 10-year period.

If skill was a meaningful factor in outperformance, the correlation would be much higher. Think of it this way. In most areas of demonstrable expertise, you would see a persistency of the skill. It's unlikely that Roger Federer will slip from his high ranking one year to competing in the qualifying rounds the next. The conclusion is inescapable that outperformance of these funds (or of any one of them) was a random, unpredictable event, unrelated to the skill of the fund manager.

Investment clubs serve many useful functions, like networking and socializing. If you are a member of one, you should understand the very nature of the activity of the group (attempting to pick mispriced stocks or find the next hot fund manager) will likely result in lower returns. You would be far better off relying on the wisdom of wise crowds.

The millions of investors all over the world looking at stock prices meet the definition of *wise crowds*. It's highly likely that their views of a fair price for a given security are accurate. Don't fight them. Join them.

What's the Point?

The judgment of all investors worldwide is wise. You should heed it.

CHAPTER 5

Trading Against
Goldman Sachs

**By the way, all of the jokes here tonight are brought to you by our
friends at Goldman Sachs. So you don't have to worry, they make
money whether you laugh or not.**

—President Barack Obama

B y this time, I hope I have convinced you there is something fundamentally wrong with the abysmal lack of ethics on Wall Street. The culture of greed has caused them to betray your interests, time and again. I have also shown why you may be subconsciously drawn like bees to honey to the entreaties of brokers who promise big rewards with scant regard to risk.

Now I want to get to the heart of the matter: Buying and selling is the lifeblood of the securities industry. They want you to buy and sell stocks, bonds, mutual funds, options, gold, and all the other financial instruments their fertile minds can dream up.

Here's the first question I want you to ask yourself before you engage in any of these transactions: Who's on the other side of the trade?

Remember this: If you are buying, someone else is selling. If you believe a stock is going up, someone else believes it is going down. When you place a trade, you are making the assumption that you know more than the person (or firm) on the other side of the trade. How confident are you of that conjecture?

Trading has become a huge portion of the profits of the brokerage and investment banking firms through whom many people are placing trades. In the first nine months of 2010, trading fees accounted for 36% of Morgan Stanley's revenues and a much higher proportion of its profits. Big Wall Street firms have major trading advantages their customers lack. They have huge resources, including both personnel and computer technology.

Whatever they are doing seems to be working. Goldman Sachs reported net earnings of $8.3 *billion* for 2010. Its net revenue in investing and lending activities was $7.54 billion.

Since you have no way of knowing whether the person on the other side of your trade is Goldman Sachs or Joe Shmoe, why are you so confident in your judgment that your trade is a good one? If you are trading because you think you are going to make a big score, keep in mind that big returns mean you are assuming big risks. Risk is a two-way street.

Trading is a very bad idea. Unlike Goldman Sachs, you won't make money no matter what happens. It's more likely you will have tears in your eyes.

What's the Point?

Don't underestimate the intelligence of those
on the other side of your trade.

CHAPTER 6

What You Can *Really* Learn from Dr. Doom

I am not going to say I told you so, but I did.

—Nouriel Roubini, professor of economics, New York University,
Stern School of Business

You are really tough. The moral turpitude of Wall Street doesn't faze you. The prospect of trading against people with far more resources and expertise doesn't scare you. You don't believe the market sets fair prices. You think you (and your broker) know more than the collective wisdom of the markets. This chapter is for you.

Your trading strategy assumes you and your broker have some predictive power, either concerning the market in general or a particular security you are about to trade. You must have this core belief since, as I have explained, today's prices reflect all current information. It's tomorrow's news that moves stock prices. There are a lot of gurus who say they know tomorrow's news. They make all kinds of predictions.

Probably the best-known market seer is Nouriel Roubini, professor of economics at New York University's Stern School of Business. He is also the chairman of Roubini Global Economics, an economic consultancy firm.

Roubini bolted into prominence by accurately predicting the crash of the housing market, which he said would "sink the economy." This prediction instantly gave him the newfound status of seer. He was courted by the financial media, and his negative predictions about the market and the economy earned him the nickname "Dr. Doom."

Flush with confidence, Roubini gave very specific advice to investors contemplating investing in the market in 2009. Here was his advice:

> For the next 12 months I would stay away from risky assets. I would stay away from the stock market. I would stay away from commodities. I would stay away from credit, both high-yield and high-grade. I would stay in cash or cash like instruments such as short-term or longer-term government bonds. It's better to stay in things with low returns rather than to lose 50% of your wealth. You should preserve capital. It'll be hard and challenging enough. I wish I could be more cheerful, but I was right a year ago, and I think I'll be right this year too.

The Dow Jones Industrial Average gained 22.68% in 2009. The S&P 500 gained 23.45%. The NASDAQ was up 43.89%. Professor Roubini was right about 2008. He was dead wrong about 2009. That's my point.

Roubini is not alone in making bad predictions. Here's one from the National Association of Realtors' former chief economist David Lereah, in November 2005. You would think you could rely on his views concerning the future of the housing markets: "The good news is that inventory levels are improving and housing supply will come closer to buyer demand in 2006. We expect a healthy and more balanced market next year." The housing market started its downward spiral in the summer of 2006.

Who knows more about the state of the economy than Federal Reserve Chairman Ben Bernanke? In March 2007, here's what he had to say about the subprime crisis: "At this juncture, however, the impact on the broader economy and financial markets of the problems in the subprime market seems likely to be contained. In particular, mortgages to prime borrowers and fixed-rate mortgages to all classes of borrowers continue to perform well, with low rates of delinquency."

After the market crash and the housing crash in 2008, Bernanke was asked to explain his faulty prediction. He dryly stated, "Of course, I would like to revise and extend my remarks."

If you need further evidence of the folly of relying on self-styled seers, consider the analysis of market timing newsletters by Jeffrey M. Laderman in *Business Week* that showed that none of them beat market returns for the 10-year period studied. These newsletters were sold to the public by people claiming to have special, valuable insights into the future. They didn't.

Rich Dad Poor Dad author Robert Kiyosaki made this prediction about the stock market for 2010: "The current stock market rally will probably turn into a dead cat bounce. If the Dow drops below 6,500, 5,000 may be the next stop." The Dow ended 2010 at 11,577. The market looked more like a raging bull than a dead cat.

Sometimes the experts are right. Sometimes they are wrong. Don't mistake luck for skill. You can't call it *skill* when you are right and *bad luck* when you are wrong. There is no data indicating anyone has predictive powers about the future—much less the future of the markets.

Here's something else about predictions you may not know: They are more likely to be correct simply as a matter of luck than you might expect. If you make 10 forecasts, and each one has a 10% probability of correctly predicting the future, there is a 65% chance that at least one of your forecasts will be correct.

When your investment strategy relies on predictions—no matter how credible the source—you are gambling, not investing.

What's the Point?

Predictions have zero reliability. Smart Investors ignore them.

CHAPTER 7

The Myth of the Lost Decade

**I've lost a bet. I've lost my keys. But I've
never lost a decade—until now.**
—Sam Stovall, chief investment strategist at
S&P Equity Research Services

The securities industry has a lot of weapons in its arsenal to keep you in its fold. One of the most potent (and misleading) is its reference to the "lost decade." The argument goes like this: The S&P 500 index was basically flat for the past decade. Investors who followed an indexing-based approach suffered as a consequence. The concept of "buy and hold" is also dead.

What's the alternative? You are told to trust your broker, who can help you through these troubled times by anticipating market corrections, investing in stocks when the market is going up, and selling them before it goes down.

The financial media, which derives significant advertising revenue from the securities industry, poured kerosene on the lost-decade fire. The *Wall Street Journal* noted that "Adjusted for inflation and dividends, the return on the S&P 500 was negative for the decade that ended on June 30 [2008]." And *Business Week* joined the fray, calling it a "decade of decay."

I had a front-row seat to the intensity of this issue when I appeared on

CNBC's *Power Lunch* on April 17, 2009. I was asked for my views about the best way to save for retirement. I said, "One of the things that you could do . . . is to give us more 'In Bogle we Trust' and much less 'In Cramer we Trust.'" (I was referring to John Bogle, the founder of Vanguard Group, and a strong proponent of index-based investing; Jim Cramer is the hyperkinetic host of the CNBC show aptly titled *Mad Money*.)

At that point in the interview, Cramer stormed onto the set and proceeded to trash index funds. Here's what he said:

> In all due respect, the S&P is flat literally for ten years. . . . That's John Bogle's world. . . . I've had it with the people who tell me about the index fund. . . . For ten years they've done nothing! For ten years! When do they get called on the carpet? When are they ever wrong? Do we have to wait another ten years? Enough of this! I've said my piece.

He then stomped off the set.

This is errant nonsense, but it does provide an opportunity to expose how Wall Street misleads you. Initially, the S&P 500 index is *not* an appropriate benchmark for the U.S. stock market. The best index for that purpose is the Wilshire 5000, which measures the performance of *all* U.S. stocks (although the performance of this broader index was also flat for the same decade).

The S&P 500 index does not include any international stocks, which should be part of any properly diversified portfolio. It also does not include a bond component, which should be included in the portfolio of most investors. From January 2000 through December 2010, the Lehman (now Barclays Capital) Aggregate Bond Index was up 96.84%, which validates the importance of holding bonds in your portfolio.

No competent adviser would recommend you put 100% of your assets in an S&P 500 index. Instead, you should be investing in a globally diversified portfolio of stock and bond index funds, with low management fees, dividing your investments among stocks, bonds, and cash, in an asset allocation suitable for you.

Assume you held a globally diversified portfolio of low management fee index funds in the allocations noted in the chart below from June 1, 1998, through June 30, 2008, with a tilt toward small and value stocks. Your approximate returns are shown in the chart:

Portfolio	Annualized Returns
Low risk (20% stocks, 80% bonds)	4.64%
Medium-low risk (40% stocks, 60% bonds)	5.70%
Medium risk (60% stocks, 40% bonds)	6.66%
Medium-high risk (80% stocks, 20% bonds)	7.52%
High risk (100% stocks)	9.20%

Let's put the data from the chart in a real-world context. If you invested $100,000 on June 1, 1998, in an asset allocation of 60% stocks and 40% bonds, and checked your balance on June 31, 2008, your $100,000 would have increased in value to $191,604.

Proponents of the lost decade are using that position to cover up their real agenda. They want you to rely on their expertise, to puff up their importance as wise counselors you should trust, and ultimately to get control of your assets so they can start trading. It's a very slippery slope, since acceptance of the lost decade means you have bought into the demonstrably false premise that these advisers can beat the markets and add value to your portfolio.

It's simply not true.

What's the Point?

Lose any adviser who talks about the lost decade.

CHAPTER 8

The Myth of the Excellent Company

In my ongoing study, now at 10 years and counting, analysts' most-favored stocks underperform the Standard & Poor's 500 Index.

—John Dorfman, financial columnist for Bloomberg

Here's what Wall Street wants you to believe. Do your research. Find "excellent companies." Invest in them. Since you don't have the resources to do this research yourself, rely on a broker or financial adviser to do it for you and follow his or her recommendations.

It seems to make so much sense. Doing research works in most other areas of human endeavor. We respect academics, scientists, and drug companies that do research. They make enormous contributions to our lives and to humankind. Surely, doing research should be the foundation that guides your investing decisions. Right?

I am not knocking all research relating to investing. The Super-Smart Portfolio is based on rigorous, peer-reviewed academic studies, which *should* form the basis for your investing decisions. My critical observations are limited to the common practice by brokers (which are well accepted by most investors) that encourages research to find mispriced stocks or fund managers who can beat the markets.

The reality is that doing research to uncover the next hot stock or mutual fund to include in your portfolio is a terrible, counterproductive idea. As I explained in Chapter 4, all information about publicly traded securities is already in the public domain and factored into the price of those securities. It's highly unlikely you or your broker is going to uncover a significant fact unknown to billions of traders looking at the same information.

Here's the real kicker: Even if you could uncover an excellent company, that doesn't mean that it would be a good investment. Every year, *Fortune* magazine does a survey titled "America's Most Admired Companies." According to *Fortune*, these companies serve as the "gold standard of corporate reputation." The methodology used by *Fortune* to identify those stellar companies is exhaustive. It combines two surveys into one. The surveys have impressive names: "America's Most Admired Company" survey and "World's Most Admired Company" survey.

Fortune's partner, the Hay Group, looked at hundreds of companies. They asked executives, directors, and analysts to rate these companies in their own industry on nine criteria, from investment value to social responsibility. The final list consists of companies admired most by their peers. For 2010, it included Apple, Google, Berkshire Hathaway, Johnson & Johnson, and Amazon. Who could quarrel with this selection?

The *Fortune* list of most admired companies gets lots of press. Many investors believe investing in these companies is a no-brainer because they accept the underlying assumption that great companies make great investments. They are wrong.

An exhaustive study published by Santa Clara University's Leavey School of Business reviewed the returns of *Fortune*'s list of most admired companies from April 1983 through December 2007. It found the stock of the admired companies had *lower* returns, on average, than the stocks of the spurned companies during this period. The difference was significant. The average annualized return of the less admired companies was 17.8% compared to 15.4% for the most admired companies.

The reason for this difference will become significant when I give you my recommendations for the SuperSmart Portfolio. It comes down to this fact: The stocks of small and value companies have higher returns over time than those of the large and growth companies (like most of the ones on the *Fortune* list).

In my view, research about companies in an effort to find stock "winners" is a waste of time and a counterproductive exercise for investors. Research that attempts to find excellent companies is even worse. Success with this useless task is a good predictor of *lower* returns.

What's the Point?

Returns for stocks in excellent companies generally aren't excellent.

CHAPTER 9

The Myth of Holding Individual Stocks

During the period from 1997 to 2003, an average investor holding
a concentrated position in a single NASDAQ 100 (or an S&P 500)
stock had the same expected return as an investor holding
the entire NASDAQ 100 (or the entire S&P 500) but was
exposed to nearly twice as much risk on average.

—Craig McCann and Dengpan Luo, financial economists

Assume you are planning a photographic safari to a remote and dangerous region in Africa. You have two choices. You can go with the most experienced guide in the region, who has been guiding tourists without incident for 30 years. The guide is provided without cost by the government to encourage tourism.

Your other option is to proceed on your own, with no guide. The government office has warned that tourists without guides may have the same experience as those with guides, except the risk of death or injury is much greater. Would you find this decision difficult?

Every day investors elect to take significantly more risk, without the benefit of additional return. They do so by purchasing individual stocks instead of diversifying their risk by buying a basket of those stocks available in index funds.

When you buy an individual stock, you own a share of stock in a real company. Let's call the company whose stock you bought Smartco. It's a financial services company, run by Phil Smart, who is known as the "Oracle of Austin" for his unique wisdom and insight into the markets. Smartco is one of the stocks that make up the S&P 500 index.

The share price of Smartco could go up or down. No one knows. As I explained in Chapter 4, the price you paid for it was a fair price, set by the collective wisdom of investors worldwide who were looking at all the publicly available data about the company.

Owning Smartco means you are undertaking risks—risks that few investors understand. But what if:

- Phil dies unexpectedly.

- Smartco gets hit by a wave of shareholder derivative lawsuits.

- The CFO of Smartco embezzles from the company and flees to Brazil.

All of these risks are unique to Smartco. They would not affect the returns of the other 499 companies in the S&P 500 index.

Why would you take this additional risk by owning only Smartco? Obviously you wouldn't, unless you believed you would be rewarded with additional returns over buying an index fund that tracks the S&P 500 index.

The reality is that the expected return of Smartco is the same as the expected return of an index fund that tracks the S&P 500 index. But by holding Smartco you are taking significantly more risk, without the expectation of additional return that you could realize by holding the index.

I am not suggesting holding the index is without risk. There are market risks that can affect all of the stocks in an index.

Why are you embarking on a trip through a remote and dangerous part of Africa without a guide? The guide is free. The destination and experience are likely to be the same. Only the risk is different.

What's the Point?

You can achieve the same expected return, with significantly less risk, by holding index funds instead of individual stocks.

CHAPTER 10

The Myth of Holding Individual Bonds

The SEC doesn't require brokers to disclose how much they make on bonds they sell to you. That ignorance can be costly.

—Alex Anderson, *Forbes* tax advantaged investor

olding individual bonds is even less wise than holding individual stocks, although some of the same reasoning applies.

A bond index fund (like a stock index fund) provides more diversification than holding individual bonds. Diversification reduces the risk of holding individual bonds, by reducing risks unique to those bonds. As you learned in the previous chapter, you are not rewarded for taking this kind of risk.

Individual bonds can default. Their credit quality can range from risky to secure. They can have other characteristics that might affect your returns.

A bond index fund has professional management responsible for managing a portfolio of billions of dollars of bonds. Your broker—regardless of his or her expertise—cannot match the experience and buying power of the major bond funds.

The world of bond trades is opaque. Few individuals have the ability to understand the real cost and commissions of the bonds purchased from their broker. According to Larry Swedroe, author of *The Only Guide to a Winning Bond Strategy You'll Ever Need*, broker dealers can add spreads of 2% to 6% on purchases and sales of bonds.

Bond funds buy and sell at wholesale prices, taking advantage of their huge buying power and superior trading expertise.

It's easier to get in and out of a bond index fund than it is to build and liquidate positions in individual bonds. One transaction is all it takes. Partial liquidations of your bond investments are much easier with bond funds because you don't have to sell an entire bond (you are simply selling shares in the bond fund).

Reinvestment is also easier with bond funds than with a portfolio of individual bonds. Bond funds are able to invest new cash and reinvest income more efficiently than you and your broker can with your portfolio of individual bonds.

As with all investments, low costs correlate with higher returns. The management fees (or expense ratios) for bond index funds are much lower than the fees for managing individual accounts. For instance, you can purchase the Vanguard Total Bond Market Index Fund (VBMFX), which has an expense ratio of only 0.22%. Fees for managing separate bond accounts can be two to three times higher.

With rare exceptions (like very high net worth investors who can purchase enough bonds to fully diversify their bond portfolio or who need or want more control over the bonds in their portfolio) you would be better off holding a bond index fund than individual bonds.

What's the Point?

Bond index funds give you more diversification, superior management, and lower costs compared to owning individual bonds.

CHAPTER 11

The Myth of Skill

Although men flatter themselves with their great actions, they are not so often the result of a great design as of chance.
—François de La Rochefoucauld

In January 2010, I created the Solin Random Stock Index (SRSI). I selected the first two stocks listed on a U.S. stock exchange that appeared for each letter of my last name. Here's the list of 10 stocks that made up the SRSI, followed by their ticker symbols:

Sprint Nextel (S)

Sirius XM Radio (SIRI)

Realty Income (O)

Oracle (ORCL)

Loews (L)

Las Vegas Sands (LVS)

Intel (INTC)

International Business Machines (IBM)

Netsuite (N)

Nvidia (NVDA)

The performance of the SRSI was dazzling. From January 2010 through November 2010, it was up an astounding 45.14%. During the same period, the S&P 500 index increased by a paltry 5.87%.

The SRSI clobbered the returns of most of the best mutual funds in the country. These funds are run by highly skilled fund managers, who have access to awesome computer power and reams of sophisticated analytical data.

The purpose of this exercise was to demonstrate that outstanding returns can be achieved by sheer luck. This was not so clear to many investors who contacted me and asked how they could invest in the SRSI!

When Wall Street pundits are right in their predictions about the direction of the market or about whether a certain stock is a good buy, they attribute their success to skill. It's most often nothing more than luck. The ability to confuse luck with skill is the key to their success in convincing you to entrust your assets to their "skilled" management. Understanding that this faux expertise is nothing more than luck is critical to your investment success.

The SRSI was a crude experiment designed to expose luck masquerading as skill. Several exhaustive studies have come to the same conclusion.

One peer-reviewed study published in the *Journal of Finance* looked at the 32-year record of 2,076 stock mutual funds. The well-credentialed authors of the study used sophisticated statistical testing to distinguish results attributable to luck from those based on skill.

The number of fund managers who beat their benchmark over time was "statistically indistinguishable from zero." The few that did were simply lucky. Professor Russ Wermers, one of the coauthors of the study, concluded that it "seems hopeless" to try to pick a mutual fund that will outperform the market.

In their study of the returns of 3,156 stock mutual funds over a 22-year period, Eugene Fama and Kenneth French (more about them later) concluded that the "vast majority" of the managers of these funds did not exhibit "skill sufficient to produce expected returns that cover the costs funds impose on investors."

Even more disheartening for investors is the difficulty of finding those few fund managers who might have enough skill to cover their costs. According to the study, "they are hidden among the mass of managers with insufficient skill."

These studies and others are powerful evidence of the lack of skill of actively managed mutual funds (where the fund manager attempts to beat a given benchmark). Yet you are probably not aware of them. If you were, you might find them difficult to fully understand and appreciate. Your broker and market-beating advisers aren't going to enlighten you about them.

Don't be fooled.

What's the Point?

Wall Street is not completely lacking in skill. It takes considerable skill to convince you it has an expertise that doesn't exist and that you should pay for this nonexistent skill.

CHAPTER 12

A Potpourri of Other Myths

Insanity: doing the same thing over and over again
and expecting different results.
—Albert Einstein

I f you still believe the myths I have debunked so far, and continue to invest the Wall Street way, you will be validating Einstein's definition of insanity. Don't expect any different result.

There are many other investing myths. They all fit neatly within the agenda of the securities industry:

- They want you to take action.

- They want you to act based on short-term information.

- They want to create fear and anxiety because that encourages you to act (and to trade and read or view the financial news).

- They want to tempt you with new products (or tout the benefits of old ones) that appear to offer increased return without additional risk.

As you will see in Part Two, this is the *opposite* of what you should do. Here's a quick review of some of the biggest investment myths.

The Myth of Gold

Anyone with an agenda can cherry-pick short-term returns and make gold look like either a great buy or a terrible investment. Some examples follow.

The spot price (the current delivery price as traded on the spot market) for gold went from $39 an ounce in 1970 to $1,391 on December 1, 2010. If you bought in 1970, and sold in 2010, gold was an exceptional investment. But what if you bought in 1950, when gold was at $40 an ounce and sold in 1970, when gold was at $39 an ounce? Your 20-year investment in gold was a loser.

Very long-term returns, adjusted for inflation, are revealing: From 1802 to 2001, $1 invested in gold would have been worth $0.98. If you invested the same dollar in stocks, you would have ended up with $599,605.

For the 48-year period from 1945 to 1992, investors in gold achieved a measly 0.1% better return than an investment in U.S. Treasury bills, but *with nine times more risk.*

A broadly diversified portfolio of stocks and bonds includes an allocation to gold and other commodities. It is difficult to understand why anyone familiar with this data would elect to overweight their portfolio in gold or to try to discern the right time to buy and sell it.

The Myth of Hedge Funds

If you believe in superheroes, you might want to buy a hedge fund. You would have to assume that the managers of these funds have cracked the code and can deliver outsized returns without additional risk. If this were true (and it isn't) you would think their methodology would be set forth in at least one peer-reviewed financial journal. In fact, it would be worthy of the Nobel Prize in Economics.

The data (which are rarely reported by the financial media) tell a far different story. In one exhaustive study, Burton G. Malkiel and Atanu

Saha, looked at a database of more than 5,500 hedge funds. They concluded that hedge funds "are far riskier and provide much lower returns than is commonly supposed."

They also observed that investors in hedge funds "take on a substantial risk of selecting a very poorly performing fund or worse, a failing one." Finally, they debunk the illusion that "fund of funds" (which are hedge funds that invest in other hedge funds run by managers believed to be exceptionally skilled) achieve superior results to the industry as a whole.

There's big money to be made in hedge funds . . . running them, not investing in them. The compensation of some fund managers is measured in billions. That's not surprising, given the fee structure. It's typically 2% of assets plus 20% of profits, giving hedge fund managers an incentive to take big risks with your money. As usual, they win, even if you lose.

Since late 2006, at least 117 hedge funds at 71 fund families have gone out of business. Nevertheless, the industry continues to thrive, with total assets under management estimated to be approximately $2.7 trillion.

The Myth of Socialism

As part of a massive rescue operation precipitated by the 2008 meltdown, the U.S. government took large ownership positions in car companies, insurance companies, and the banking industry. The involvement of the government in the economy is viewed by some as an unwelcome trend away from traditional capitalism and a warning to investors about the perils of investing in a socialist economy. The data tell a different story.

For the 10 years ending December 31, 2008, and the 39 years ending December 31, 2008, the annualized stock market returns of "socialist" countries (like Norway, Denmark, Hong Kong, Sweden, and France), those in which the governments curtail economic freedom, *exceeded* the annualized returns of the United States.

It appears there is an *inverse* relationship between higher returns and economic freedom. It's equally clear that government intervention is not a precursor to lower returns.

The Myth of the New Normal

Dr. Mohamed El-Erian is the CEO of PIMCO, an asset manager with more than $1.2 trillion under management.

El-Erian coined the term *new normal* to describe what he believes are fundamental changes to the global economy. According to El-Erian, in the new normal global economy, India, China, and Brazil will have more influence, and the United States and Germany will have less, due to slower growth in the economies of the latter countries. This somewhat obvious observation has caused many investors to believe it would be prudent to sell their U.S. stocks and invest in these fast-growing emerging markets.

As usual, the data tell quite a different story from the one widely disseminated in the financial press. Historically, returns are abnormally *higher* after a recession and not lower. In the last 10 recessions in the United States, stocks increased in value by an average of 32% one year after the market low.

Investing only in high-growth countries is a *bad* idea. Countries with higher-growth economies tend to experience lower expected returns than do countries with lower-growth prospects. This is exactly the opposite of what you are led to believe.

While investing in high-growth countries has some surface appeal, the reality is the price of stocks in those countries already takes into consideration their prospects for economic growth. GDP growth is only one of many factors in determining stock returns. You can find countries with high growth and low returns as well as the reverse.

For investors, there is no new normal.

The Myth of Principal-Protected Notes

Principal-protected notes are sold as guaranteeing 100% of your investment, as long as you hold them to maturity. They are linked to varying underlying investments, typically indexes, individual stocks, or baskets of specific stocks. These notes are presented as a win–win for investors. Supposedly, the amount you invest is fully protected, and if the underlying investments do well, you benefit from that appreciation in value.

These investments were anything but a win for holders of principal-protected notes issued by Lehman Brothers. They lost more than $1 billion when the firm collapsed.

Sales of principal-protected notes are booming, with estimates as high as $34 billion sold in 2009. Yet few investors understand they risk total loss if the issuer goes out of business. The reality is that the only principal with real protection are the fees generated by the brokerage firms selling the notes.

There are other problems with these complex instruments. About a third of your investment is typically invested in low-risk investments. It is this money that will grow over the term of your investment (5–10 years is typical) to pay you back your principal. You are essentially funding your own protection and limiting your upside since only the balance of two thirds or so of your investment is actually invested in the underlying securities where the potential payoff really lies.

High fees also reduce your returns. These fees are typically in excess of 7% and frequently include a percentage of profits.

When you have even a modest understanding of how this investment really works, you will conclude that the primary beneficiaries (as usual) are the issuers of the notes, and the brokers who sell them with great enthusiasm. You as the investor are most likely to lock yourself into a long-term investment with little or no growth.

The Myth of Private Equity Funds

I have reviewed hundreds of private equity deals, most of which are structured as limited partnerships in which the private equity firm acts as the general partner. Accredited investors fund the investment(s) of the partnership.

One factor was very consistent: The general partner, and often its affiliates, made off like bandits (an appropriate reference). The investors' returns were quite modest and often nonexistent.

The sad fact is that these partnerships are set up to benefit everyone but those who invest in them. Lawyers, vendors, brokers, promoters . . . the list of those taking fees is endless. Maybe these investments should be called *limited return* partnerships, which would be a far more accurate way to describe them.

Because most limited partnerships don't disclose their financial results, reliable performance data are difficult to ascertain. One study by Steve Kaplan and Antoinette Schoar looked at a data set of returns based on voluntary reporting of limited partnerships from 1980 to 2001. The study found that average returns, net of fees, were "roughly equal" to the S&P 500 index. You can bet that those limited partnerships that declined to disclose their financial results were likely far below average.

Another study had more sobering findings. The authors, Ludovic Phalippou and Oliver Gottschalg, concluded that the average performance of private equity funds, net of fees, was 3% a year *below* that of the S&P 500 index. Fees were a whopping 6% a year, which tells you why private equity deals are sold so enthusiastically.

You can buy Vanguard's S&P 500 Index Fund (VFINX) with an expense ratio of only 0.17%. This fund will always track the returns of the S&P 500 index, less its very low management fees. Why would you pay 6% in fees, with the likelihood of significantly underperforming this index, and have the added burden of illiquidity, among other risks?

By some estimates, in 2008, $181 billion was invested globally in private equity deals and more than $90 billion was invested in 2009. The fact that so many sophisticated investors could be persuaded to put their money into these deals that make little economic sense is a testament to the awesome selling power of the securities industry.

As you review these investing myths, note the common feature: high fees. High fees nicely summarizes the raison d'être of Wall Street.

What's the Point?

Ignore market theories and investments that encourage you to do anything other than to invest in a globally diversified portfolio of low management fee index funds in an asset allocation suitable for you.

CHAPTER 13

The Cost of Believing Investing Myths

It is very hard, if not impossible, to justify active management if your goal is to grow wealth. If, instead, you view active management as a source of entertainment, you may wish to consider less costly ways to amuse yourself.

—Mark Kritzman, president and CEO, Windham Capital Management

Most investors have no idea how much active management is costing them. There are a number of studies that quantify the overall cost of this ill-advised investment practice.

One study, titled "Measuring the True Cost of Active Management by Mutual Funds," found the "real" cost to investors for all the funds tracked by a major database was 5.2% a year, which is far higher than the published expense ratios. The author of the study took into consideration the fact that actively managed funds contain mostly stocks in the index they track, and actively manage only a relatively small portion of the overall portfolio. The 5.2% cost was the cost investors are paying to have that small portion of the fund actively managed.

A more recent study, titled "The Cost of Active Investing," compared the cost of active versus passive investments. The author of the study concluded that active investors (which include approximately 90% of individual investors) could have increased their average annual return by 0.67% over the 1980–2006 period by simply switching from an active to a passive portfolio. By some estimates, engaging in the futile effort to beat the markets costs investors approximately $80 billion a year.

Translation: Most of you are paying big bucks for lower returns.

If you had a spigot pouring $80 billion into your pocket every year, would you do anything to turn it off? Of course not. Wall Street has that spigot. It uses its massive advertising budget to keep it flowing freely. It does so by perpetuating many of the myths I have discussed and by creating a climate of fear and uncertainty to keep you coming back for more.

One of the more insidious tricks of the trade to keep the spigot flowing freely is known as the *closet index fund*—mutual funds for which the fund manager purchases most of the stocks in the index he or she is supposed to beat. These funds charge high fees for portfolios that consist primarily of the same stocks that make up the benchmark index they are tracking. In effect, you are paying 100% (or more) in higher fees for a fund that is likely to underperform an index fund, with significantly lower management fees.

Closet index funds are anything but a minor player in the mutual fund industry. One study found "a significant fraction" of the largest (more than $1 billion in assets) funds are closet indexers.

In Part Two, you will have the satisfaction of learning how to turn off the spigot . . . permanently.

What's the Point?

The fees charged by active fund managers who are usually engaged in the futile effort to "beat the markets" reduces returns by $80 billion a year.

The Smartest Way

To evaluate the Smartest Portfolios and select the one that is right for you, you need to accept the underlying premise that capturing the returns of the global stock and bond markets is a superior way to invest. Knowledge of risk, rebalancing, and the effect of taxes are also critical to investing successfully.

CHAPTER 14

Superior Returns Are Within Your Grasp

Stand clear and keep your eye on the ball
—W. C. Fields

Financial advisers, scholars, and others who study the financial markets debate endlessly about how many angels fit on the head of a pin. In their search for the best portfolio, they focus on matters that mean little, and ignore those that would have a major effect on your returns.

Here's where your focus should be: Until you accept the fact that capturing the returns of the global stock and bond markets yields superior returns, you will probably spend your investing life enriching your broker or wealth adviser at your expense. Just say no to:

- Market timing

- Buying individual stocks or bonds

- Actively managed mutual funds

- Alternative investments

- Variable annuities

- Equity indexed annuities

- Private equity deals

- Principal-protected notes

- Currency trading

- Commodities trading

We don't need to debate how the focus on active management has worked for the average stock investor. Studies show that over a 20-year period ending December 31, 2009, the average stock mutual fund investor earned only 3.17%, while the S&P 500 index returned 8.20%. When you consider inflation and taxes, the average stock fund investor lost money. It would not be difficult to improve that dismal performance.

The first issue you need to decide is whether you are going to continue down a path that has been so demonstrably unsuccessful over time or whether you will fundamentally change the way you invest. Once you elect to make the change, the rest is easy.

Let's assume you had become an index-based investor in January 1990. Instead of actively managing your stock portfolio, you purchased an index fund that tracked the Russell 3000 Index, which represents approximately 98% of the U.S. stock market. For the 20-year period through December 31, 2009, you would have earned an annualized return of 8.34%, less the low fees and costs for the index fund you purchased.

Compare that return to the 3.17% return earned by the average investor, who was moving in and out of actively managed stock funds, trying to beat the markets, probably with the encouragement of a broker. That's why the right focus should be on capturing market returns.

The Smartest Portfolios, based on historical data, are likely to increase your returns compared to other index-based portfolios. But any globally diversified portfolio of low management fee stock and bond index funds in an asset allocation suitable for you is vastly superior to active management of your investments.

What's the Point?

The overwhelming data demonstrate that index-based investing is superior to active management.

CHAPTER 15

The Right Focus

It's a fact: you can positively impact only one aspect of investment performance—your allocation of assets among broad asset classes. Stock or mutual fund picking and market timing, the things traditionally thought to be critical to investment success, turn out to be almost irrelevant. How can this be?
—William J. Bernstein, financial theorist and author

A seminal study published in 1986 titled "Determinants of Portfolio Performance" by G. P. Brinson, L. R. Hood, and G. L. Beebower should have changed the way you invest. Unfortunately, you probably never heard of it.

This study found that the asset allocation of a portfolio (the division between stocks, bonds, and cash) is the primary determinant of the variability of your returns (the potential range of outcomes). Stock picking and market timing are relegated to minor concerns.

Most of your conversations with your broker are probably about stock picking and market timing. They should be focused on your asset allocation. Fortunately, determining the right asset allocation for you is not difficult.

There are many asset allocation questionnaires in books and on the Internet that can help you make this determination. I have one on my website, which is short and very reliable. You can take it online at www.smartestinvestmentbook.com.

It's important for you to understand how these questionnaires are structured so you can appreciate the factors that determine your asset allocation. There are only three relevant issues:

How long will it be before you are likely to need 20% or more of invested assets?

What is the worst one-year loss you would tolerate before pushing the "sell now" button?

How much risk do you need to take?

The Smartest Portfolios permit you to select from the following risk levels:

- Low risk (20% stocks, 80% bonds)

- Medium-low risk (40% stocks, 60% bonds)

- Medium risk (60% stocks, 40% bonds)

- Medium-high risk (80% stocks, 20% bonds)

- High risk (100% stocks, 0% bonds)

55/45 (ᴏᴏʀ CHOICE)

The following guidelines will help you determine which portfolio is right for you:

Low risk (20% stocks, 80% bonds). You have a minimum of 4 years before you will need 20% or more of your funds. If a 5% loss in any one year would cause you to dump this portfolio, it's not for you. Unless you meet both of these criteria, you should have no exposure to the stock market. You should confine your investments to FDIC-insured savings accounts, Treasury bills, and high-quality money market funds from major fund families like Vanguard or Fidelity (which carry slightly more risk).

Medium-low risk (40% stocks, 60% bonds). You have a minimum of 6 years before you will need 20% or more of your funds. If a 15% loss in any one year would cause you to dump this portfolio, it's not for you.   7 YRS ; 20% LOSS MAX ACCEPTABLE

Medium risk (60% stocks, 40% bonds). You have a minimum of 8 years before you will need 20% or more of your funds. If a 25% loss in any one year would cause you to dump this portfolio, it's not for you.

Medium-high risk (80% stocks, 20% bonds). You have a minimum of 12 years before you will need 20% or more of your funds. If a 35% loss in any one year would cause you to dump this portfolio, it's not for you.

High risk (100% stocks, 0% bonds). You have a minimum of 15 years before you will need 20% or more of your funds. If a 45% loss in any one year would cause you to dump this portfolio, it's not for you.

When considering the amount of risk you should take, remember that bigger is not always better.

A 35-year-old entrepreneur approached me several years ago. He had just sold his company for $25 million. He reviewed data indicating that, over the long term, more exposure to stocks has generated higher returns. He wanted to invest in a high-risk portfolio. He explained that he had a very long time horizon before he would need any of these funds.

The data supported his selection: $25 million invested 20 years ago in one of our portfolios of passively managed funds, allocated 80% to stocks and 20% to bonds, would have been worth almost $160 million at the end of 2010. He liked those numbers!

I explained to him that if he had made this investment on January 1, 2008, it would have lost approximately $8 million that year. I asked him if he had the stomach to wait out that kind of loss. Then I asked him why he needed to take so much risk. There is a big difference between being able to afford risk and needing to take it. Jason Zweig, a highly respected financial journalist and author, put it this way: "Thou shalt take no risk that thou needest not take."

I recommended a far more conservative portfolio, consisting of 30% stocks and 70% bonds. If he had invested in that portfolio 20 years ago, it would be worth $90 million at the end of 2010. In 2008, that portfolio lost $2.35 million—a big difference from the $8 million loss for the high-risk portfolio in that year.

While the $70 million difference in ending values is significant, I asked him how having $90 million instead of $160 million would change his life. At some point, it obviously makes no difference at all. I then explained that long-term historical data are very good but are not predictive. There is always the possibility of a "black swan" event, which would make all predictions meaningless.

Black swan is a term coined by Nassim Nicholas Taleb in his book of the same name. It is used to explain hard-to-predict, rare events, beyond the realm of normal expectations. A terrorist attack on a major city and a destructive massive earthquake (like the one that recently occurred in Japan) are examples of black swan events. If a black swan event occurred, it could (but might not) dramatically affect the worst historical loss numbers.

This is the kind of analysis you need to do before selecting the risk level of your portfolio. You can keep pace with inflation very nicely with a low-risk portfolio. If that's all the risk you need to incur, don't take more risk just because you can afford it.

In the ideal world, you would locate the right portfolio for you and not look at it again for at least the minimum holding period (other than to rebalance). The more aggressive your portfolio (meaning the more exposure you have to stocks rather than bonds), the greater short-term volatility it will experience. It's critically important to understand that the trade-off for greater long-term returns is increased short-term volatility.

Here's what the market is saying to you: "I understand you want to maximize your long-term returns. That's fine with me, but here's the price I am going to extract. You must endure short periods of stomach-churning losses. If you can wait out those times and stick to your minimum holding period, there is a strong likelihood I will uphold my end of the bargain."

If you can't cope, then select a more conservative portfolio. There will still be short-term volatility, but the range will be far narrower.

What's the Point?

Your tolerance for risk is driven by your time horizon and your tolerance for short-term volatility.

CHAPTER 16

Taxes and Costs: Stealth Enemies

But why, oh why, do managed mutual funds as a group seem to go out
of their way to have their shareholders pay the highest taxes possible?
—Bill Barker, financial journalist

ere's a question that will stun the most glib broker into extended
silence: What are the *after-tax* returns of the actively managed
funds in my portfolio?

Mutual funds report returns on a before-tax basis. The reason is simple: Actively managed funds buy and sell far more frequently than index funds. Index funds buy or sell only when necessary to track the index.

Buying and selling results in either short- or long-term capital gains. You have to recognize these gains and pay taxes on them. The less frequently your mutual funds buy and sell, the lower the realized gains. Lower realized gains means less taxes you have to pay.

The difference in returns is stunning. John Bogle studied the tax effects on returns of actively managed versus index funds from 1980 through 2005. He found index fund investors earned higher returns and paid only a fraction of the taxes paid by investors in actively managed funds. Note that $10,000 invested in the average actively managed stock fund was worth $108,000 before taxes; however, when taxes were considered, that amount shrank dramatically to $71,000.

Compare those results to the experience of the index investor over the same time period. The same investment in an S&P 500 index fund returned $181,000 before taxes and $158,000 after taxes. The active investor incurred a 33% tax hit. The index investor paid a little under 13% in taxes.

Another study by Joel Dickson and John Shoven looked at 147 funds from 1963 to 1992. The authors found investors paid more than $1 billion in extra taxes over what they would have had to pay in a tax-efficient fund. They also found that using after-tax performance data instead of pre-tax data caused a dramatic change in fund performance rankings.

ETFs: Even More Tax Efficient

All of the Smartest Portfolios recommended in this book consist of low-cost index funds or exchange-traded funds (ETFs). ETFs are funds that track an index but can be traded like a stock. A study by Morningstar found that ETFs were generally more tax efficient than comparable mutual funds. Like index funds, ETFs track benchmarks, which reduce the turnover in their portfolios. As we have seen, lower turnover means lower taxes.

When you sell an ETF, you sell it in the market through a broker. It's not redeemed by the ETF sponsor. This means the sponsor doesn't have to sell shares (and create taxable gains) when you decide to sell an ETF. With mutual funds, redemptions by the shareholders in a mutual fund can sometimes force mutual fund managers to sell shares of their underlying securities, causing you to incur capital gains and pay taxes.

Large investors who want to sell their ETFs will often deal directly with the ETF sponsor. The sponsor will exchange shares of the underlying stocks in the ETF portfolio in lieu of cash, which also reduces taxable transactions.

The news about ETFs isn't all rosy. Unlike index funds, you can't buy an ETF directly from the fund sponsor. You will need to open a brokerage account, which will expose you to all the sales pitches and gimmicks employed by those firms.

Trading costs are higher for ETFs. You may have to pay a commission and incur the "bid-ask spread"—the difference between the highest buyer's price and the lowest seller's price—each time you buy or sell an ETF. When you buy an ETF, you will pay the ask price. When you sell an ETF, you will receive the bid price.

In the Smartest Portfolios, I recommend only large, liquid ETFs, which tend to have the smallest bid-ask spreads.

Recently, Charles Schwab, Vanguard, iShares, and TD Ameritrade began programs offering commission-free trades on certain ETFs. Be sure to check the rules for each firm before placing a transaction. Some firms limit commission-free transactions to ETFs that they sponsor.

While index funds permit you to automatically reinvest your dividends, which is very convenient, most brokers do not permit automatic reinvestments of dividends from ETFs. However, many (like Vanguard) have a no-fee, no-commission reinvestment program if you are reinvesting in the same securities. Nevertheless, reinvesting on your own requires more attention to the buildup of cash in your account and the need to appropriately invest this cash.

This bears repeating: Avoid all calls from brokers at the firms you decide to use to purchase your ETFs. They will try their best to lead you astray!

What's the Point?

You can lose a substantial portion of your total return to taxes when you invest in actively managed funds.

CHAPTER 17

Rebalancing: Sense and Nonsense

The returns differences among various rebalancing strategies are quite small in the long run.
—William J. Bernstein, financial theorist and author

Rebalancing is a way to ensure your portfolio is no more or less risky than you intend. Both have adverse consequences. For example, if the stock portion of your portfolio increases in value by more than the bond portion, you have a riskier portfolio than the one you created because the allocation to stocks is now higher. The solution is simple: Sell some of the stocks and buy more bonds to bring your asset allocation back to its initial level.

Unfortunately, what sounds simple in theory can be quite daunting in practice.

The first issue is inertia.

Most investors either never rebalance or make few changes to their portfolios. If you fell into this category, you experienced adverse consequences in 2008 when the markets tanked. The run-up of stocks that preceded the crash overweighted your portfolio in stocks. When stocks fell, your portfolio experienced more losses (perhaps much more) than it would have if you had rebalanced to keep your original allocation between stocks and bonds in place.

There are many theories of rebalancing, and that's precisely the problem. The options are confusing, and you are likely to throw up your hands and do nothing. Here are some suggestions I have heard:

1. **Rebalance periodically.** Some suggest rebalancing semiannually.

2. **Rebalance when asset classes are out of whack.** If an asset class deviates from its original allocation by more than a set percentage, rebalance.

3. **Rebalance when the markets are volatile.** In turbulent markets, move from high-risk to lower-risk assets.

4. **Rebalance based on expected market conditions.** Make changes based on where you think the market is headed.

Options 3 and 4 make absolutely no sense since they require you to predict the unpredictable. Options 1 and 2 have surface appeal, but there remain a lot of variables, like timing and percentages that should trigger rebalancing.

There are other rebalancing issues you need to consider.

Remember, rebalancing involves transaction costs. You will be buying some funds and selling others. If the funds are ETFs, you may pay commissions and the bid-ask spread. Commissions will vary, depending on your broker. Generally, transaction costs are to be avoided—or at least minimized—because they reduce returns.

In a taxable account, rebalancing can trigger long- or short-term capital gains, which also reduce returns.

As a practical matter, what is needed is a moderate, simple approach to rebalancing, which removes the inertia barrier and encourages investors to maintain an appropriate level of risk.

A study by Vanguard concluded that annual or semiannual monitoring of your portfolio, and "rebalancing at 5% thresholds, produces an acceptable balance between risk control and cost minimization." The study also advised that implementing your rebalancing strategy by redirecting interest income, dividends, new contributions, and withdrawals was optimal.

Three of the four Smartest Portfolios (each of which contains five risk levels from which you can choose) require rebalancing. Vanguard's recommendations seem like a commonsense, easy-to-implement rebalancing approach. The Smartest Target Date Portfolio automatically rebalances.

What's the Point?

Rebalancing once or twice a year—when your allocations alter your risk level by more than 5%—makes sense.

PART THREE

The Smartest Portfolios

There are four Smartest Portfolios. The SuperSmart Portfolio is based on the groundbreaking research of Eugene F. Fama and Kenneth R. French. It may not be suitable for every investor, so I offer three alternative Smartest Portfolios. One of them is likely to be the optimal choice for most investors.

CHAPTER 18

The Four Smartest Portfolios: An Overview

On balance, the financial system subtracts value from society.
—John C. Bogle, author and founder of the Vanguard Group

I wish I could give one "Smartest" Portfolio that is right for everyone. Unfortunately, this is not possible.

Instead, there are four Smartest Portfolios. Within each portfolio, there are the five risk levels (low risk, medium-low risk, medium risk, medium-high risk, and high risk). One of the Smartest Portfolios, and one of the risk levels in one of those portfolios, is likely to be right for you. Risk and return data are provided for each risk level of each of the Smartest Portfolios. Finally, the historical results of all four Smartest Portfolios, at each risk level, are compared.

1. **The SuperSmart Portfolio** is based on the Fama-French three-factor model that sets forth three key elements that explain the risk and return of diversified portfolios: the percent invested in stocks (market), the amount of small company stocks (size), and the amount of value stocks (value). Made up of nine funds in specific allocations (seven funds in the high-risk allocation), the SuperSmart Portfolio is constructed based on factors that have

proven to correlate positively with maximizing returns for a given level of risk.

2. **The Smartest Target Date Portfolio** involves the purchase of one fund. It typically has a date in its name, which is the date when you are likely to retire (like the Vanguard Target Retirement 2045 Fund [VTIVX]). Each year, the target fund becomes more conservative, gradually shifting from stocks to bonds. No rebalancing is required. If you can't handle the SuperSmart Portfolio *and* if the allocation in the risk level you require in the Smartest Target Date Portfolio is right for you, it could be a very simple answer to your investing concerns.

3. **The Smartest ETF Portfolio** involves the purchase of three exchange-traded funds. It gives you total flexibility to allocate the percentage of stocks and bonds in your portfolio, but it limits your ability to allocate between domestic and international stocks.

4. **The Smartest Index Fund Portfolio** involves the purchase of three index funds from Vanguard, Fidelity, or T. Rowe Price. It's the portfolio recommended in my previous books. It gives you maximum flexibility to allocate your funds between U.S. and international stocks. It also gives you broad exposure to the investment-grade U.S. bond market, but it does not give you exposure to the international bond market. It also does not take advantage of the Fama-French research concerning the benefit of tilting your portfolio toward small company and value stocks. It has withstood the test of time, having performed extremely well during the recent tumultuous markets.

What's the Point?

Any of the four Smartest Portfolios is likely to yield vastly superior returns when compared to active management.

CHAPTER 19

Fama and French Are SuperSmart

The theory essentially says that if you want better returns you can get them by going for smaller companies and value stocks.
—Travis Morien, Australian investment adviser and financial journalist

The SuperSmart Portfolio is based on the research of two distinguished professors of finance: Eugene F. Fama and Kenneth R. French. Fama is a professor of finance at the University of Chicago Booth School of Business. His earliest exposure to the financial markets was working part-time for a stock market newsletter firm while he was a student at Tufts University. His job was to locate "signals" that would tell investors when to buy and when to sell stocks. He was frustrated by his inability to predict market trends or to locate indicators that would permit him to do so.

After graduating from Tufts, he was awarded his doctorate at Chicago Booth. In 1965, he published his thesis, titled "Random Walks in Stock Market Prices." His theory, which came to be known as the efficient market hypothesis (EMH), holds that since information about publicly traded securities is available to everyone at about the same time, one cannot beat the markets consistently without purchasing riskier investments.

Efforts to beat the market through technical analysis or studying fundamentals (like earnings and asset values) do not overcome this barrier to achieving outsized returns. Fama concluded that stock prices were random and efficient and that the work of chartists and others engaged in fundamental analysis (studying financial information relating to the sales and operations of a company) was of little to no value in consistently making better-than-chance predictions of stock prices.

Consider the significance of this conclusion: Almost a half century ago, Fama basically was telling the securities industry that the entire premise of their value proposition to their clients (their ability to pick stock winners or to predict the direction of the markets) had no basis in scientific fact. While others had posited the same theory earlier, Fama was the first one to support it with rigorous academic research.

In 1992, Fama, and his coauthor on many of his most memorable scholarly papers, Kenneth R. French, determined the factors that explain the relationship between investment risk and return for stocks. Knowing what factors accounted for returns, a portfolio could be structured to maximize returns while being adequately compensated for the level of risk taken.

This model is enormously significant. Understanding it will permit you to fundamentally change the way you invest. Instead of following notions discredited by Fama (and by hundreds of academic studies), your investments will be based on sound academic research. This is the same research used by the most sophisticated investment advisers in the world to invest trillions of dollars of assets.

I don't want to leave you with the impression that the Fama-French three-factor model is universally accepted. However, the factor model they identified as being the source of risk and return continue to be the gold standard among Nobel Prize laureates in economics and others who study the capital markets.

Before you take a leap of faith with such an important decision, a brief review of the academic research behind the composition of the SuperSmart Portfolio is in order. The three factors that make up what is known as the Fama-French three-factor model are as follows:

1. **The market factor:** The percent of your portfolio invested in stocks compared with the percentage of your portfolio invested in bonds.

2. **The size factor:** The amount of small company stocks (where the market value of outstanding shares is between $300 million and $2 billion) in your portfolio.

3. **The value factor:** The amount of value stocks (where the stock price is low compared to the fundamentals like sales and earnings) in your portfolio.

Not all these variables are equal in weight. By far, the most important one is market risk (the allocation of your portfolio to stocks), which accounts for about 70% of the performance of your overall portfolio (for better or worse). Over time, the higher your exposure to stocks, the greater your returns are likely to be, compared to U.S. Treasury bills, which are considered to be risk-free investments. The percent of small company and value stocks in your portfolio accounts for approximately 26% of your returns. The balance of 4% remains unexplained.

Distilled to its essence, the Fama-French three-factor model holds that a portfolio tilted toward small and value stocks is likely to outperform a portfolio without this tilt, over the long term. Small and value stocks are riskier asset classes than are large and growth stocks. Investors have been rewarded over the long term for the additional risk in investing in them.

The three-factor model applies to only the stock portion of your portfolio. There are two additional factors that explain most of the returns in the bond portion. I will explain those factors after I discuss the three factors applicable to stocks in more detail.

The Market Factor

The market factor is based on this premise: The higher the percentage of stocks (compared to bonds) in your portfolio, the higher the return.

Investment in stocks is riskier than investment in U.S. Treasury bills and investment-grade bonds. You are rewarded over the long term for taking on this additional risk. Over the short term, you can be punished by market volatility and short-term losses.

The Size Factor

The size factor is based on this premise: The more exposure you have to small company stocks, the higher your returns are likely to be when compared to a portfolio of large company stocks.

The term *small size stocks* refers to relatively small companies with a market capitalization of between $300 million and $2 billion. *Market capitalization* is the total dollar value of all of a company's outstanding shares. To calculate it, you take the total number of outstanding shares and multiply it by the current market price of one share. You won't need to do this calculation since I will include the names of the funds that benchmark this asset class when I provide the recommended funds you should purchase if you decide to use the SuperSmart Portfolio.

Small companies are riskier than are large companies. Investors in riskier asset classes are rewarded over the long term for taking on the additional risk.

French has compiled data, which can be found on his website's home page (http://mba.tuck.dartmouth.edu/pages/faculty/ken.french), comparing the returns of small versus large company stocks. From

December 31, 1926, to December 31, 2008, the annualized return of small companies was 11.28% compared to an annualized return of 9.89% for large companies.

The difference of 1.39% per year may not seem significant, but it is. If $10,000 is invested for 10 years earning 11.28% a year, it is worth $29,118 at the end of the 10-year period. That same $10,000 invested for 10 years earning 9.89% a year is worth $25,679 at the end of the 10-year period. That's a difference of $3,439 on an investment of $10,000.

The additional return from adding small stocks to your portfolio is not without risk. There can be extended periods of time when small company stocks underperform large company stocks. For example, from 1969 to 1974, small company stocks underperformed large company stocks. The periods of high and low performance can be significant and prolonged.

The Value Factor

The value factor is based on this premise: The more exposure you have to value company stocks, the higher your returns are likely to be when compared to a portfolio of growth company stocks.

By *value stocks*, Fama and French are referring to stocks the market has priced lower than its fundamentals might otherwise warrant. Value stocks have a high *book-to-market value ratio*. This is a fancy way of saying they are low priced compared to their underlying value. Here is the way this calculation is done:

The *book value* of a company is calculated by determining its net worth, which is simply its assets minus its liabilities. This term is often referred to on a firm's balance sheet as "stockholder's equity."

The *market value* of a company is calculated the same way you determine its market capitalization—that is, multiply the number of shares outstanding by the current market price of the stock.

To get the *book-to-market ratio*, divide the book value of the firm (its net worth) by its market value.

As a general guideline, if the book-to-market ratio is above 1, the stock would be considered potentially undervalued and thus a value stock. If it is below 1, it would be considered potentially overvalued and thus a growth stock. The ratio of 1 is somewhat arbitrary. A more precise way to identify value stocks would be based on the overall value of all firms in the market. Those that have a ratio above the average would be considered value stocks, whether or not the average is 1.

You can find the book value (net worth) of a company from the balance sheet of the company's filings with the Securities and Exchange Commission. Its share price can be found on Yahoo! Finance and on many other finance sites.

Here's a simple example: A company has a book value of $10 million. It has one million shares of outstanding stock, with a current market price of $20, making its market value $20 million. Make the calculation: $10 million divided by $20 million equals 0.5. This company is not a value stock.

If the current market price of its stock was $5, its market value would be $5 million. Its book-to-market ratio would be 2.0 ($10 million divided by $5 million equals 2.0), and it would be considered a value stock. Value stocks are riskier than growth stocks in bad economic times, and slightly less risky when times are good. Over the long term, you are rewarded for taking on this additional risk.

The data from French's website shows that from December 31, 1926, through December 31, 2008, value stocks had an annualized return of 12.26%, compared to an annualized return of 8.91% for growth stocks. The difference was 3.35% a year. Using the same $10,000 hypothetical investment, for the same 10-year period, the difference is $8,309.

As with small company stocks, there can be prolonged periods of time when value stocks underperform growth stocks. For example, from August 2006 to November 2009, growth beat value on a two-year rolling basis. Think of these periods as the punishment you have to suffer for having a portfolio that is likely to yield higher returns for the risk taken over the long term.

You don't have to worry about identifying value stocks or doing any of these calculations. The funds that benchmark the value segment of the market are identified as part of the discussion about the SuperSmart Portfolio.

The Bond Factors

Now that you understand the three factors that determine the variability of returns in the stock portion of your portfolio, let's look at the bond portion. Most portfolios (for all but those with the longest time horizons) will consist of a mix between stocks and bonds.

You need to be concerned only about these two variables:

Term: Bonds with terms of five years or less are optimal.

Default risk: You want bonds with a very low likelihood of defaulting.

The specific bond funds that meet these criteria are set out in the recommendations for all the portfolios in this book.

To summarize, three factors determine the variability of returns in the stock portion of your portfolio:

- Market exposure

- Small company stock exposure

- Value company stock exposure

Two factors determine the variability of returns in the bond portion of your portfolio:

- Term of the bond

- Default risk

These five factors determine almost all the variability of the returns in a diversified portfolio of stocks and bonds.

Until recently, it was not possible to construct a portfolio with publicly traded funds using the Fama-French three-factor model, which all investors could access, without using a broker or adviser. However, that's precisely what the SuperSmart Portfolio has been designed to do, using index funds and exchange-traded funds.

What's the Point?

You can now engineer a portfolio to maximize expected returns and properly compensate you for the risk you undertake.

CHAPTER 20

The SuperSmart Portfolio: Designed to Produce Higher Returns

The three-factor model allows investors to engineer equity portfolios to capture additional returns derived from priced risk factors.
—Frank Armstrong, registered investment adviser

The SuperSmart Portfolio has been structured in a way that rewards you (to the extent possible) with the maximum expected return for the risk you are taking. It was created by following four simple principles.

1. Minimize risk by including seven different asset classes for stocks and two asset classes for bonds for each risk level. This provides for broad diversification across asset classes where the returns are unlikely to correlate with each other.

2. Divide the stock portion of the portfolio for each level of risk between domestic and foreign stocks: 70% to domestic and 30% to foreign stocks. This provides for a globally diversified portfolio, further reducing risk.

Although international stocks account for about 50% of global market capitalization, when factors like currency volatility, increased transaction costs, and a trend toward higher correlations between foreign and domestic markets are considered, an allocation range of 20% to 40% of foreign stocks is likely to capture most of the benefits of diversification. The 30% allocation recommended for the SuperSmart Portfolio strikes a nice balance.

3. Follow the Fama-French three-factor model. The SuperSmart Portfolio is tilted toward small size and value stocks, which increases the potential to earn higher returns for the amount of additional risk taken.

4. Optimize the trade-off between risk and return by using a customized program to run calculations based on what is known as the Sharpe ratio.

The Sharpe ratio, named after its creator, Nobel Laureate William Sharpe, indicates how much return a given investment provides over a risk-free investment, such as a short-term Treasury bill, while adjusting for the incrementally greater risk over the risk-free investment. It's important because if you are not being compensated for taking on additional risk over a risk-free investment, why would you do so?

Just because a portfolio delivers a higher return than another portfolio doesn't mean it is a better portfolio. The higher return may be the result of taking more risk, which means a greater possibility of loss. The Sharpe ratio tells you how much a portfolio (or a mutual fund) returned, in relation to the amount of risk it took.

When comparing two or more investments, the higher the Sharpe ratio, the better the relationship between the risk you are taking and the expected return of your investment. The Sharpe ratio should be used with some caution because it is calculated based on historical returns, which are not necessarily predictive of future results. When combined with the other principles used to created the SuperSmart Portfolio, it is a useful tool but not one on which you should place total reliance. (More information about the Sharpe ratio, and a specific example of how it is calculated, is provided in Chapter 33.)

What's the Point?

The SuperSmart Portfolio builds on the research of Fama and French and uses the Sharpe ratio to create a portfolio that maximizes returns for a given level of risk.

CHAPTER 21

The SuperSmart Portfolio: Chapter and Verse

A smart man makes a mistake, learns from it, and never makes that
mistake again. But a wise man finds a smart man and learns from
him how to avoid the mistake altogether.

—Roy H. Williams, author and marketing consultant

The SuperSmart Portfolio consists of nine index and exchange-traded funds (seven if you select the high-risk asset allocation). If you want to adopt it, just follow these four steps:

1. Open a brokerage account.

2. Determine your asset allocation.

3. Purchase the funds in the SuperSmart Portfolio for your risk level.

4. Rebalance periodically.

Purchasing and rebalancing nine funds is fairly easy, but it's not for everyone. Maybe the amount you have to invest is too small to justify owning this number of funds or you want a portfolio in which reinvestment of dividends is easier or that rebalances automatically, or you just don't want to open a brokerage account. If you fall into any of these categories, then one of the other Smartest Portfolios would be a better option.

For all allocations other than the high-risk one, the SuperSmart Portfolio has an allocation to seven stock funds and two bond funds. The amount of your portfolio allocated to stocks and bonds is a critical decision that will have the most significant impact on your expected returns.

The stock portion of the SuperSmart Portfolio has the same percentage exposures to seven stock asset classes. This exposure is as follows:

20% U.S. large cap

20% U.S. large value

20% U.S. small value

10% U.S. real estate

10% international value

10% international small

10% emerging markets

There is no incrementally higher exposure to emerging market small or emerging market value, although it might have been optimal to include them. It's difficult to benchmark these indexes, and the only ETFs that attempt to do so don't have significant assets under management. The exclusion of these asset classes will not significantly affect the performance of this portfolio.

The fixed-income portion of the portfolio is divided evenly between a short-term U.S. government and a short-term foreign (non-U.S.) government portfolio.

The SuperSmart Portfolio consists of stock and bond funds from Vanguard and iShares based on a determination that those funds were the most tax efficient, with the lowest expense ratios.

While it is not necessary for you to fully understand how the allocations were determined, for those who want to delve deeper, here's some additional information.

Reasonable people can differ over the percentage of small and value stocks that should be in a portfolio based on the Fama-French three-factor model. Without a tilt toward value, you would expect that 50% of the stocks in a broadly diversified stock portfolio would be value stocks and 50% would be growth stocks. In the Super-Smart Portfolio, 80% of the stocks are value stocks and only 20% are growth.

Similarly, you would expect to see 90% of the stocks in a broadly diversified stock portfolio to be large company stocks and only 10% small size stocks. In the SuperSmart Portfolio, 66% are large and 33% are small.

The tilt toward value and small could have been greater or less than what is specified and still be consistent with the Fama-French three-factor model.

THE SUPERSMART PORTFOLIO

Fund	Low Risk	Medium- Low Risk	Medium Risk	Medium- High Risk	High Risk
Vanguard Large Cap Index Admiral Fund (VLCAX)	4.0%	8.0%	12.0%	16.0%	20.0%
Vanguard Value Index Admiral Fund (VVIAX)	4.0%	8.0%	12.0%	16.0%	20.0%
Vanguard Small Cap Value ETF (VBR)	4.0%	8.0%	12.0%	16.0%	20.0%
Vanguard REIT Index Admiral Fund (VGSLX)	2.0%	4.0%	6.0%	8.0%	10.0%
iShares MSCI EAFE Value ETF (EFV)	2.0%	4.0%	6.0%	8.0%	10.0%
iShares MSCI EAFE Small Cap ETF (SCZ)	2.0%	4.0%	6.0%	8.0%	10.0%
Vanguard Emerging Markets Stock Index Admiral Fund (VEMAX)	2.0%	4.0%	6.0%	8.0%	10.0%
iShares Barclays Short Treasury Bond ETF (SHV)	40.0%	30.0%	20.0%	10.0%	0.0%
SPDR Barclays Capital Short-Term International Treasury Bond ETF (BWZ)	40.0%	30.0%	20.0%	10.0%	0.0%

This is a breakthrough, do-it-yourself portfolio that is suitable for many investors. It empowers every investor to invest in a portfolio previously available through only a limited number of investment advisers based on cutting-edge financial research. Although there are many reasons why you should consider retaining such an adviser (discussed in Part Five), for those investors with the discipline to purchase and rebalance these funds, this information will permit you to achieve optimal returns for the amount of risk you elect to take.

What's the Point?

If you can handle purchasing and rebalancing as many as nine
funds, the SuperSmart Portfolio is worthy of serious consideration for
do-it-yourself investors.

CHAPTER 22

SuperSmart Portfolio Returns

Although it is always perilous to assume that the future will be like the past, it is at least instructive to find out what the past was like.
—William F. Sharpe, winner of the 1990 Nobel Memorial Prize in Economic Sciences

L ong-term historical data are not predictive of future returns, but they are the best source on which we can rely. Risk and return data for the SuperSmart Portfolio are provided for the following periods (all ending in 2010): 20 years, 10 years, 5 years, and 3 years. As the time period measured gets shorter, you should view the data with greater skepticism.

Because the markets were so tumultuous in the 2008–2010 time period, I am including data for that period so you can see how the SuperSmart Portfolio performed under very unusual market conditions. Again, remember: This is *very* short-term data. Risk and return sources are set forth in Appendix B.

The decision about the level of risk you select will be based on the results of your asset allocation questionnaire. Younger investors, with longer time horizons, can have more exposure to stock market risk.

Older investors, with a more limited time horizon, should have a more conservative portfolio, with less exposure to stocks and a larger percentage of bonds in their portfolio.

SUPERSMART PORTFOLIO: RISK AND RETURN 20 YEARS

ALL PERFORMANCE DATA ARE EXPRESSED IN PERCENT AND ARE HYPOTHETICAL INVESTMENT RESULTS FOR THE PERIOD 1991–2010.

Measure	Low Risk	Medium-Low Risk	Medium Risk	Medium-High Risk	High Risk
Average annual return (geometric)	6.17	7.53	8.75	9.82	10.72
Annualized standard deviation	4.44	7.45	10.90	14.48	18.11
Worst single-calendar-year period	−3.45	−12.39	−21.33	−30.27	−39.21
Worst two-calendar-year period	3.44	−7.06	−17.37	−27.50	−37.43
Worst three-calendar-year period	9.27	3.29	−4.31	−13.49	−23.16

SUPERSMART PORTFOLIO: RISK AND RETURN 10 YEARS

ALL PERFORMANCE DATA ARE EXPRESSED IN PERCENT AND ARE HYPOTHETICAL INVESTMENT RESULTS FOR THE PERIOD 2001–2010.

Measure	Low Risk	Medium-Low Risk	Medium Risk	Medium-High Risk	High Risk
Average annual return (geometric)	5.17	5.98	6.54	6.85	6.85
Annualized standard deviation	5.04	9.36	14.14	19.05	24.00
Worst single-calendar-year period	−3.45	−12.39	−21.33	−30.27	−39.21
Worst two-calendar-year period	3.44	−7.06	−17.37	−27.50	−37.43
Worst three-calendar-year period	9.27	4.38	−4.31	−13.49	−23.16

SUPERSMART PORTFOLIO: RISK AND RETURN 5 YEARS

ALL PERFORMANCE DATA ARE EXPRESSED IN PERCENT AND ARE
HYPOTHETICAL INVESTMENT RESULTS FOR THE PERIOD 2006–2010.

Measure	Low Risk	Medium-Low Risk	Medium Risk	Medium-High Risk	High Risk
Average annual return (geometric)	4.96	5.28	5.28	4.89	4.07
Annualized standard deviation	5.01	10.69	16.62	22.60	28.60
Worst single-calendar-year period	−3.45	−12.39	−21.33	−30.27	−39.21
Worst two-calendar-year period	3.44	−7.06	−17.37	−27.50	−37.43
Worst three-calendar-year period	9.27	4.38	−4.31	−13.49	−23.16

COVERS
2008 RECESSION

SUPERSMART PORTFOLIO: RISK AND RETURN 3 YEARS

ALL PERFORMANCE DATA ARE EXPRESSED IN PERCENT AND ARE
HYPOTHETICAL INVESTMENT RESULTS FOR THE PERIOD 2008–2010.

Measure	Low Risk	Medium-Low Risk	Medium Risk	Medium-High Risk	High Risk
Average annual return (geometric)	3.00	2.78	2.06	0.78	−1.15
Annualized standard deviation	5.95	14.11	22.29	30.48	38.66
Worst single-calendar-year period	−3.45	−12.39	−21.33	−30.27	−39.21
Worst two-calendar-year period	4.39	0.46	−4.64	−10.91	−18.35
Worst three-calendar-year period	9.27	8.58	6.31	2.36	−3.41

In reviewing the returns for the risk levels of the SuperSmart Portfolio, the following become obvious:

- Higher risk was reflected in higher returns and higher short-term volatility.

- Low standard deviation numbers correlated with lower risk and lower volatility.

- Higher standard deviation numbers correlated with higher risk and higher volatility.

- Even the lowest-risk portfolio (held for five years or more) yielded returns far in excess of the historical annual rate of inflation which is 3.03%.

- All returns are pre-tax.

What's the Point?

The SuperSmart Portfolio has yielded historical returns for a given level of risk that validates the research of Fama and French.

Smartest Alternative Portfolios

In the following chapters, I provide three alternative portfolios: the Smartest Target Date Portfolio, the Smartest ETF Portfolio, and the Smartest Index Fund Portfolio. One of the three alternative Smartest Portfolios may be your best choice. While each is unique, the portfolios in Part Four have many things in common with the SuperSmart Portfolio:

- They require you to determine your asset allocation.
- They are index based.
- They are globally diversified.
- The underlying index funds and ETFs have low management fees.

Because each of the Smartest Portfolios share the same underlying characteristics that reflect Smart Investing, you really can't go wrong even though they don't take full advantage of the Fama-French research.

CHAPTER 23

The Smartest Target Date Portfolio

Investors simply pick a retirement date, say, 2020 or 2030, and hit cruise control.

—Daren Fonda, financial journalist

The first of the three alternative portfolios, the Smartest Target Date Portfolio, is also the easiest to understand and to own.

The asset allocation decision is the primary determinant of the volatility of your investments (described as the "variability of returns") over time. However, most investors don't have an asset allocation appropriate for them. If they do, it often drifts due to market changes, and they end up taking too much or too little risk. Target date funds (TDFs) help solve this problem with the minimum amount of participation from the investor.

Introduced in 1994, TDFs have enjoyed rapid growth. By some estimates, more than $256 billion were invested in them at the end of 2009, with Fidelity Investments and Vanguard being the biggest players with more than 60% of the market.

With a TDF, you simply select a fund with the date closest to when you intend to retire, and the fund does the rest. It automatically adjusts its stock and bond allocation each year to become more conservative. It requires no active rebalancing.

The basic principles for selecting an optimal TDF are very straightforward:

- The initial asset allocation should be appropriate for you.

- The evolution of the fund to become more conservative over time should be based on sound principles of investing.

- All of the underlying funds should be index funds with low management fees.

- The underlying stock funds should be globally diversified.

- The underlying bond fund should track an index that represents investment-grade bonds, such as the Barclays Capital Aggregate Bond Index.

The asset allocation in a given TDF may not be right for everyone who is going to retire on or about the date established by the fund. If you have a $10 million trust account (lucky you!), you may want a more aggressive allocation to stocks than someone who is living paycheck to paycheck. That's why it's very important to look at the initial and ongoing asset allocation in the TDF you are considering.

If the asset allocation in the TDF you are considering is not right for you, then consider one of the other Smartest Portfolios. Asset allocations in TDFs (both the initial asset allocation and the manner in which they become more conservative over time) are fixed by the fund manager. You have no control over them.

If the asset allocation is appropriate, then go down the checklist of basic principles above to be sure the TDF you select meets each of these criteria. Currently, only one fund family appears to meet all of them: Vanguard.

As of this writing, Vanguard's target date funds (which are called target retirement funds) reduce exposure to stocks from 90% for those retiring in 2050 to less than 60% for those retiring in 2015. The high exposure to stocks in the 2050 fund reflects the long time horizon of those in their twenties. The exposure to stocks for those about to retire may be too aggressive for you, so be sure you are comfortable with that level of risk.

The underlying funds are all Vanguard *index* funds, with low management fees averaging only 0.20%. The stock funds are globally diversified.

The bond fund provides broad exposure to U.S. investment-grade bonds. It invests 70% of its assets in U.S. government bonds of all maturities.

And finally, the minimum investment is reasonable: $3,000 initially and $100 for additional investments.

Note that the Smartest Target Date Portfolio does not have a tilt toward small and value, which Fama and French believe maximizes returns for the level of risk taken. To get that tilt, you need to adopt the SuperSmart Portfolio.

Target Date Funds: Risk and Return

Evaluating performance data for target retirement funds is tricky because they are a moving target, whereas the other three Smartest Portfolios have static asset allocations. Target retirement funds evolve from aggressive to conservative over time. For example, the Vanguard Target Retirement 2015 Fund (VTXVX) has an asset allocation of approximately 60% stocks and 40% bonds. However, five years ago it was more aggressively invested in stocks, and five years from now it will have a larger component of bonds.

Taking into account that the morphing aspect of target retirement funds affects both returns and volatility (as measured by standard deviation), the chart below shows the pre-tax, average annual returns for the Vanguard Target Retirement 2015 Fund as of December 31, 2010, as reported on the company's website.

1 year	12.47%
3 year	1.19%
5 year	4.42%
Since inception (September 27, 2003)	5.72%

Currently, Vanguard is the only option if you want a target date retirement fund that meets all of my requirements. However, other fund families are moving in the direction of copying the investor-friendly features in Vanguard's target date funds.

Fidelity recently unveiled its Fidelity Freedom Index funds. These are target date retirement funds for which the underlying funds are all index funds. As of the writing of this book, they are only available to corporate retirement plans, but that may change in the future. TIAA-CREF also has a lineup of Lifecycle Index Funds, but they are also currently available only through retirement plans.

If you are wondering why these large fund families aren't currently offering individual investors target date retirement funds in which the underlying funds are all index funds, just follow the money. The expense ratios for Fidelity Freedom Index funds and TIAA-CREF's Lifecycle Index Funds, which have actively managed underlying funds and are available to individual investors, is about 0.74% and 0.65%, depending on the fund selected. (Compare those percentages to Vanguard's at less that 0.20%). If investors are willing to pay more for a fund that yields less than its index counterpart, why offer a lower-cost, indexed-based one?

The chart below is a comparison of the performance and expense ratios (which are management fees deducted from returns) of Fidelity's Freedom 2020 Fund, TIAA-CREF's Lifecycle 2020 Fund, and Vanguard's Target Retirement 2020 Fund.

Fund	Expense Ratio	Total Return (%)*
Fidelity Freedom 2020	0.74%	17.01%
TIAA-CREF Lifecycle 2020	0.93%	15.06%
Vanguard Target Retirement 2020	0.18%	20.66%

*Total return from July 1, 2006, through December 31, 2010.

While these data are short term, for the period for which a comparison could be made, the less expensive Vanguard Target Retirement 2020 outperformed the more expensive actively managed Fidelity and TIAA-CREF funds. This trend is likely to continue in the future given the higher management fees of TIAA-CREF and Fidelity funds.

It is curious that investors are willing to pay more for a TDF that is likely to underperform comparable funds with lower management fees. Vanguard founder John Bogle noted this anomaly when he said, "Investors have paid a staggering cost for the excessive expenses and excessive marketing focus of the mutual fund industry."

What's the Point?

TDFs are a simple way to place your investments on cruise control, but they should be selected only if their asset allocation is suitable and if the underlying funds are low management fee index funds.

CHAPTER 24

The Smartest ETF Portfolio

*In oneself lies the whole world and if you know how to look and learn,
the door is there and the key is in your hand. Nobody on earth can give
you either the key or the door to open, except yourself.*
—Jiddu Krishnamurti, Indian writer and speaker on philosophical and
spiritual issues

Exchange-traded funds (ETFs) are funds that track designated indexes. They are bought and sold on stock exchanges and can be traded only through a stockbroker. Think of them as index funds that can be bought and sold like stocks.

The first goal of the Smartest ETF Portfolio is to own a globally diversified selection of stocks and bonds. This used to be very difficult. It no longer is.

The Stock Portion

There are two ETFs from which you can choose that cover the entire world of stocks:

Vanguard Total World Stock Index ETF (VT) holds 2,791 stocks, which is significant because its competitors hold only a sampling of the stocks in the index. The benchmark is the FTSE All-World Index, which is made up of 2,774 stocks from developed and emerging countries, including the United States. The Vanguard Total World Stock Index ETF has a low expense ratio of 0.30%. Although it was only recently introduced, it has assets of $1 billion. If you purchase Vanguard ETFs in a Vanguard brokerage account, there are no commissions, and you can elect to have dividends automatically reinvested.

iShares MSCI ACWI Index Fund (ACWI) is the other all-world ETF worthy of consideration. Its benchmark tracks the MSCI All Country World Index, which consists of approximately 2,400 securities across 45 markets. This index measures stock market performance of developed and emerging markets. However, iShares ETF holds only 918 of the 2,400 securities.

There are some differences between the Vanguard Total World Stock Index ETF and the iShares MSCI ACWI Index Fund worthy of note:

- The expense ratio of the iShares ETF is 0.35% versus 0.30% for the Vanguard Total World Stock Index ETF.

- The iShares ETF holds only 918 of the 2,400 stocks in the MSCI All Country World Index. Vanguard holds all of the stocks (and a few others) in the index it benchmarks.

- The iShares ETF, which was also recently introduced, has $1.5 billion in assets.

On balance, I believe the Vanguard ETF has a slight edge, but you won't go wrong with the iShares fund. Both give you a very easy way to capture the global returns of the stock market by owning one fund.

Domestic and Foreign Stock Allocations

There is a final issue to be considered if you are contemplating purchasing an all-world ETF for the stock portion of your portfolio. You need to understand the allocation in that ETF between domestic (U.S.) stocks and foreign stocks. As I noted previously, the SuperSmart Portfolio allocates 70% to domestic stocks and 30% to international, which I believe is ideal (although others have expressed the view that closer to 50% for each would be optimal).

Vanguard's ETF holds only 45% of its portfolio in U.S. stocks. The balance of 55% is held in emerging markets, Europe, and the Pacific. The iShares ETF holds only 41% of its portfolio in U.S. stocks. The balance of 59% is invested outside the United States.

If you are comfortable with this relatively high allocation of your stock portfolio invested outside the United States, these two all-world ETFs are a simple and effective way to get exposure to the world's stock market by purchasing just one fund. If you aren't, then consider the Smartest Index Fund Portfolio, which gives you the flexibility to allocate any designated percentage of your stock portfolio between domestic and foreign stocks.

The Bond Portion

You will recall in the SuperSmart Portfolio we used two bond funds: iShares Barclays Short Treasury Bond ETF (SHV) and the SPDR Barclays Capital Short-Term International Treasury Bond ETF (BWZ). An equal allocation between domestic and foreign bonds takes into consideration the fact that the U.S. bond market share has dropped from 49% to 38% of the total world bond market.

There are several benefits of exposure to international bonds, including the following:

- **Less risk:** Foreign bonds will not be affected in the same way as U.S. bonds by interest rate changes in the United States. Holding both foreign and U.S. bonds can reduce volatility since the two are not highly correlated.

- **Higher returns:** You should not be surprised to learn that historical returns from foreign government bonds have been higher than from U.S. government bonds. U.S. bonds have less risk of default, so the U.S. government does not have to offer as high an interest rate as foreign governments, where the default risk is higher.

- **Currency hedge:** Since foreign bonds pay interest and principal in the currency of the issuing country, they act as a hedge on U.S. currency.

There are also risks of holding foreign bonds, which include currency risk (if the dollar strengthens against the foreign currency, the payments received from foreign bond holdings would be reduced) and default risk, since foreign government bonds are generally riskier than U.S. government bonds.

The Smartest ETF Portfolio

If you decide to implement the Smartest ETF Portfolio, here's what you should do:

1. Invest 100% of your stock portfolio in either the Vanguard Total World Stock Index ETF (VT) or the iShares MSCI ACWI Index Fund (ACWI).

2. Invest 50% of your bond portfolio in the iShares Barclays Short Treasury Bond ETF (SHV) to gain exposure to the domestic bond market. Invest the other 50% of your bond portfolio in the SPDR Barclays Capital Short-Term International Treasury Bond ETF (BWZ) for exposure to the international bond market.

3. Rebalance annually or semiannually.

The chart below shows the composition of the Smartest ETF Portfolio at the different risk levels:

THE SMARTEST ETF PORTFOLIO

THIS PORTFOLIO DOES NOT HAVE A TILT TOWARD SMALL AND VALUE, WHICH FAMA AND FRENCH BELIEVE MAXIMIZES RETURNS FOR THE LEVEL OF RISK TAKEN. TO GET THAT TILT, YOU NEED TO ADOPT THE SUPERSMART PORTFOLIO.

Fund	Low Risk	Medium-Low Risk	Medium Risk	Medium-High Risk	High Risk
Vanguard Total World Stock Index ETF (VT) or iShares MSCI ACWI Index Fund (ACWI)	20.0%	40.0%	60.0%	80.0%	100.0%
iShares Barclays Short Treasury Bond ETF (SHV)	40.0%	30.0%	20.0%	10.0%	0.0%
SPDR Barclays Capital Short-Term International Treasury Bond ETF (BWZ)	40.0%	30.0%	20.0%	10.0%	0.0%

Risk and Return Data

The charts below provide the risk and return data for the recommended portfolio for 20-, 10-, 5-, and 3-year periods ending 2010. The sources are set forth in Appendix B. Risk and return data assumes the use of the Vanguard Total World Stock Index ETF (VT) for the stock portion of the portfolio.

THE SMARTEST ETF PORTFOLIO: RISK AND RETURNS 20 YEARS

ALL PERFORMANCE DATA ARE EXPRESSED IN PERCENT AND ARE HYPOTHETICAL INVESTMENT RESULTS FOR THE PERIOD 1991–2010.

Measure	Low Risk	Medium-Low Risk	Medium Risk	Medium-High Risk	High Risk
Average annual return (geometric)	5.68	6.54	7.25	7.77	8.09
Annualized standard deviation	4.70	7.92	11.56	15.31	19.11
Worst single-calendar-year period	−4.02	−13.53	−23.04	−32.55	−42.06
Worst two-calendar-year period	−0.21	−7.04	−15.80	−24.73	−34.85
Worst three-calendar-year period	3.01	−9.24	−20.51	−30.83	−40.25

THE SMARTEST ETF PORTFOLIO: RISK AND RETURN 10 YEARS

ALL PERFORMANCE DATA ARE EXPRESSED IN PERCENT AND ARE
HYPOTHETICAL INVESTMENT RESULTS FOR THE PERIOD 2001–2010.

Measure	Low Risk	Medium-Low Risk	Medium Risk	Medium-High Risk	High Risk
Average annual return (geometric)	4.52	4.66	4.54	4.13	3.38
Annualized standard deviation	5.22	9.64	14.51	19.49	24.52
Worst single-calendar-year period	−4.02	−13.53	−23.04	−32.55	−42.06
Worst two-calendar-year period	2.54	−6.85	−15.80	−24.73	−34.85
Worst three-calendar-year period	7.22	4.50	−1.77	−10.75	−20.59

THE SMARTEST ETF PORTFOLIO: RISK AND RETURN 5 YEARS

ALL PERFORMANCE DATA ARE EXPRESSED IN PERCENT AND ARE
HYPOTHETICAL INVESTMENT RESULTS FOR THE PERIOD 2006–2010.

Measure	Low Risk	Medium-Low Risk	Medium Risk	Medium-High Risk	High Risk
Average annual return (geometric)	4.90	5.15	5.06	4.56	3.57
Annualized standard deviation	5.49	11.13	17.02	22.97	28.95
Worst single-calendar-year period	−4.02	−13.53	−23.04	−32.55	−42.06
Worst two-calendar-year period	3.46	−4.98	−14.78	−24.73	−34.85
Worst three-calendar-year period	7.22	4.50	−1.77	−10.75	−20.59

THE SMARTEST ETF PORTFOLIO: RISK AND RETURN 3 YEARS

ALL PERFORMANCE DATA ARE EXPRESSED IN PERCENT AND ARE
HYPOTHETICAL INVESTMENT RESULTS FOR THE PERIOD 2008–2010.

Measure	Low Risk	Medium-Low Risk	Medium Risk	Medium-High Risk	High Risk
Average annual return (geometric)	2.35	1.48	0.09	−1.89	−4.56
Annualized standard deviation	6.00	14.17	22.36	30.55	38.75
Worst single-calendar-year period	−4.02	−13.53	−23.04	−32.55	−42.06
Worst two-calendar-year period	3.46	−1.42	−7.48	−14.72	−23.14
Worst three-calendar-year period	7.22	4.50	0.27	−5.56	−13.07

What's the Point?

A portfolio of three ETFs could be the smartest portfolio for you, but
pay attention to the allocation to international stocks in the all-world
stock ETFs.

CHAPTER 25

The Smartest Index Fund Portfolio

The true secret of giving advice is, after you have honestly given it, to be perfectly indifferent whether it is taken or not and never persist in trying to set people right.

—Hannah Whitall Smith, author and activist in the women's suffrage and temperance movements

In my 2006 book, *The Smartest Investment Book You'll Ever Read,* I recommended a globally diversified portfolio designed to capture stock and bond market returns. I recommended the specific index funds readers should purchase to achieve the goal of becoming Smart Investors. That advice remains as relevant today as it did then. It has proven its worth through the greatest market crash and subsequent recovery in 50 years.

The Smartest Index Fund Portfolio is very simple to understand and implement, consisting of only three index funds from Vanguard, Fidelity, or T. Rowe Price. In this portfolio, 70% of your stock allocation is in the domestic stock index fund, and 30% is in the international fund. You can adjust those percentages if you want more (or less) international exposure.

Note that the Smartest Index Fund Portfolio does not have a tilt toward small and value, which Fama and French believe maximizes returns for the level of risk taken. To get that tilt, you need to adopt the SuperSmart Portfolio.

The chart below shows the composition of the Smartest Index Fund Portfolio using funds from Vanguard at the different risk levels. (To use funds from Fidelity or T. Rowe Price, see the charts in Appendix C.)

THE SMARTEST INDEX FUND PORTFOLIO

Fund	Low Risk	Medium-Low Risk	Medium Risk	Medium-High Risk	High Risk
Vanguard Total Stock Market Index (VTSMX)	14.0%	28.0%	42.0%	56.0%	70.0%
Vanguard Total International Stock Index (VGTSX)	6.0%	12.0%	18.0%	24.0%	30.0%
Vanguard Total Bond Market Index (VBMFX)	80.0%	60.0%	40.0%	20.0%	0.0%

40% STOCK
60% BOND

Risk and Return Data

The charts below provide the risk and return data for the recommended portfolio for 20-, 10-, 5-, and 3-year periods ending 2010. The sources are set forth in Appendix B.

THE SMARTEST INDEX FUND PORTFOLIO: RISK AND RETURN 20 YEARS

ALL PERFORMANCE DATA ARE EXPRESSED IN PERCENT AND ARE HYPOTHETICAL INVESTMENT RESULTS FOR THE PERIOD 1991–2010.

Measure	Low Risk	Medium-Low Risk	Medium Risk	Medium-High Risk	High Risk
Average annual return (geometric)	7.39	7.95	8.36	8.61	8.66
Annualized standard deviation	5.64	8.34	11.69	15.27	18.95
Worst single-calendar-year period	−3.79	−12.63	−21.47	−30.32	−39.16
Worst two-calendar-year period	3.17	−6.04	−15.30	−24.61	−33.99
Worst three-calendar-year period	10.58	−1.21	−15.03	−27.51	−38.71

THE SMARTEST INDEX FUND PORTFOLIO: RISK AND RETURN 10 YEARS

ALL PERFORMANCE DATA ARE EXPRESSED IN PERCENT AND ARE
HYPOTHETICAL INVESTMENT RESULTS FOR THE PERIOD 2001–2010.

Measure	Low Risk	Medium-Low Risk	Medium Risk	Medium-High Risk	High Risk
Average annual return (geometric)	5.58	5.39	4.96	4.29	3.33
Annualized standard deviation	4.26	8.86	13.60	18.38	23.16
Worst single-calendar-year period	−3.79	−12.63	−21.47	−30.32	−39.16
Worst two-calendar-year period	3.17	−6.04	−15.30	−24.61	−33.99
Worst three-calendar-year period	10.58	3.46	−4.27	−12.60	−21.54

THE SMARTEST INDEX FUND PORTFOLIO: RISK AND RETURN 5 YEARS

ALL PERFORMANCE DATA ARE EXPRESSED IN PERCENT AND ARE
HYPOTHETICAL INVESTMENT RESULTS FOR THE PERIOD 2006–2010.

Measure	Low Risk	Medium-Low Risk	Medium Risk	Medium-High Risk	High Risk
Average annual return (geometric)	5.83	5.71	5.30	4.58	3.47
Annualized standard deviation	5.66	10.98	16.32	21.68	27.03
Worst single-calendar-year period	−3.79	−12.63	−21.47	−30.32	−39.16
Worst two-calendar-year period	3.17	−6.04	−15.30	−24.61	−33.99
Worst three-calendar-year period	10.58	3.46	−4.27	−12.60	−21.54

THE SMARTEST INDEX FUND PORTFOLIO: RISK AND RETURN 3 YEARS

ALL PERFORMANCE DATA ARE EXPRESSED IN PERCENT AND ARE
HYPOTHETICAL INVESTMENT RESULTS FOR THE PERIOD 2008–2010.

Measure	Low Risk	Medium-Low Risk	Medium Risk	Medium-High Risk	High Risk
Average annual return (geometric)	4.92	3.68	2.03	−0.09	−2.75
Annualized standard deviation	7.84	15.10	22.35	29.61	36.86
Worst single-calendar-year period	−3.79	−12.63	−21.47	−30.32	−39.16
Worst two-calendar-year period	6.76	1.35	−4.96	−12.15	−20.23
Worst three-calendar-year period	15.51	11.45	6.21	−0.27	−8.03

Choosing any one of the four Smartest Portfolios, based on historical data, would provide returns far superior to those who rely on brokers and advisers and engage in discredited active trading strategies. It's hard to stand by with indifference and see nest eggs decimated by an entire industry devoid of ethics, conscience, and, most significantly, expertise.

What's the Point?

A globally diversified portfolio of three low management fee index funds has stood the test of time and market turbulence.

CHAPTER 26

The Bottom Line

Wise are those who learn that the bottom line doesn't always have
to be their top priority.

—William Arthur Ward, motivational speaker

am not suggesting the bottom line should (or should not) be your top priority. However, when it comes to investing, it's important for you to understand the numbers.

Here's what the risk and return data tell you about the three Smartest Portfolios for which it makes sense to compare the data: the Super-Smart Portfolio, the Smartest ETF Portfolio, and the Smartest Index Fund Portfolio. Risk and return for the Smartest Target Date Portfolio were not included because these funds change over time, so it's not possible to do an apples-to-apples comparison with the other Smartest Portfolios.

For each time period, the returns for each risk level for each of the three Smartest Portfolios are set forth, followed by the standard deviation at each risk level. You will be able to easily compare both returns and risk. When viewing these data, keep in mind that past returns are not predictive. Specifically, remember that a black swan event (that rare, unpredictable occurrence that could have a dramatic impact on the markets) could produce dramatically different returns in the future.

Average annual return (geometric) takes into account the fact that the returns you earn in one year affect what you earn in subsequent years because returns are compounded over time. It is a much more accurate way to express returns than using an arithmetic annual return, which is simply the sum of a series of return observations, divided by the number of return observations.

Standard deviation is also very important. It is a measure of the volatility of the portfolio. Think of it as measuring the risk of the portfolio.

Finally, you will note some statistical anomalies in the short-term return data for some of the Smartest Portfolios. These anomalies are caused, in part, by the fact that the historical return data uses annual returns and annual rebalancing of the model portfolios to return them to their original asset allocation. When returns are very volatile, annual rebalancing can result in moderate-risk portfolios delivering higher returns than either low- or high-risk portfolios.

20 YEARS (1991–2010)

AVERAGE ANNUAL RETURN (GEOMETRIC)

Fund	Low Risk	Medium-Low Risk	Medium Risk	Medium-High Risk	High Risk
SuperSmart Portfolio	6.17	7.53	8.75	9.82	10.72
Smartest ETF Portfolio	5.68	6.54	7.25	7.77	8.09
Smartest Index Fund Portfolio	7.39	7.95	8.36	8.61	8.66

ANNUALIZED STANDARD DEVIATION

Fund	Low Risk	Medium-Low Risk	Medium Risk	Medium-High Risk	High Risk
SuperSmart Portfolio	4.44	7.45	10.90	14.48	18.11
Smartest ETF Portfolio	4.70	7.92	11.56	15.31	19.11
Smartest Index Fund Portfolio	5.64	8.34	11.69	15.27	18.95

You can appreciate the SuperSmart Portfolio when you view these results. It was the winner in three of the risk categories and runner-up in the other two. It did so by taking *less* risk (as measured by its lower standard deviation) at those respective risk levels than the other portfolios.

Higher returns, at a lower risk, are the holy grail of investing.

At the more conservative risk levels, the Smartest Index Fund Portfolio was the winner, but note that the SuperSmart Portfolio was the runner-up, taking slightly less risk.

In all categories, the Smartest ETF Portfolio came in last, which has some significance because this is the longest period measured.

10 YEARS (2001–2010)

AVERAGE ANNUAL RETURN (GEOMETRIC)

Fund	Low Risk	Medium- Low Risk	Medium Risk	Medium- High Risk	High Risk
SuperSmart Portfolio	5.17	5.98	6.54	6.85	6.85
Smartest ETF Portfolio	4.52	4.66	4.54	4.13	3.38
Smartest Index Fund Portfolio	5.58	5.39	4.96	4.29	3.33

ANNUALIZED STANDARD DEVIATION

Fund	Low Risk	Medium- Low Risk	Medium Risk	Medium- High Risk	High Risk
SuperSmart Portfolio	5.04	9.36	14.14	19.05	24.00
Smartest ETF Portfolio	5.22	9.64	14.51	19.49	24.52
Smartest Index Fund Portfolio	4.26	8.86	13.60	18.38	23.16

A similar pattern repeats itself for the 10-year period: The Super-Smart Portfolio prevails in four of the five risk levels. The risk level it took to achieve those returns was very close to the risk level of the other portfolios. The Smartest Index Fund Portfolio takes second place overall, with the Smartest ETF Portfolio again coming in last.

I don't want you to read too much into a comparison of returns for the five- and three-year periods because of their short duration. With that caveat in mind, they are shown in the charts that follow:

5 YEARS (2006–2010)

AVERAGE ANNUAL RETURN (GEOMETRIC)

Fund	Low Risk	Medium-Low Risk	Medium Risk	Medium-High Risk	High Risk
SuperSmart Portfolio	4.96	5.28	5.28	4.89	4.07
Smartest ETF Portfolio	4.90	5.15	5.06	4.56	3.57
Smartest Index Fund Portfolio	5.83	5.71	5.30	4.58	3.47

ANNUALIZED STANDARD DEVIATION

Fund	Low Risk	Medium-Low Risk	Medium Risk	Medium-High Risk	High Risk
SuperSmart Portfolio	5.01	10.69	16.62	22.60	28.60
Smartest ETF Portfolio	5.49	11.13	17.02	22.97	28.95
Smartest Index Fund Portfolio	5.66	10.98	16.32	21.68	27.03

For the five-year period, the results are mixed. The overall winner is the Smartest Index Fund Portfolio, which prevailed in three of the five risk levels. The SuperSmart Portfolio was the runner-up. The Smartest ETF Portfolio came in third in four of the five risk levels.

3 YEARS (2008–2010)

AVERAGE ANNUAL RETURN (GEOMETRIC)

Fund	Low Risk	Medium- Low Risk	Medium Risk	Medium- High Risk	High Risk
SuperSmart Portfolio	3.00	2.78	2.06	0.78	−1.15
Smartest ETF Portfolio	2.35	1.48	0.09	−1.89	−4.56
Smartest Index Fund Portfolio	4.92	3.68	2.03	−0.09	−2.75

ANNUALIZED STANDARD DEVIATION

Fund	Low Risk	Medium- Low Risk	Medium Risk	Medium- High Risk	High Risk
SuperSmart Portfolio	5.95	14.11	22.29	30.48	38.66
Smartest ETF Portfolio	6.00	14.17	22.36	30.55	38.75
Smartest Index Fund Portfolio	7.84	15.10	22.35	29.61	36.86

For the three-year period, the SuperSmart Portfolio prevailed in three of the risk categories. The Smartest Index Fund Portfolio was the runner-up in three of those categories, and prevailed in two others. The Smartest ETF Portfolio came in third in each category.

What the Comparison Means to You

Remember this comparison does not include data on the Smartest Target Date Portfolio because that portfolio shifts over time from more aggressive to more conservative, which makes a meaningful comparison impossible. Don't forget to consider the Smartest Target Date Portfolio if the asset allocation is suitable for you.

As among the SuperSmart Portfolio, the Smartest ETF Portfolio, and the Smartest Index Fund Portfolio, based solely on the numbers, the SuperSmart Portfolio was the overall winner, followed closely by the Smartest Index Fund Portfolio. The Smartest ETF Portfolio came in last.

If you can deal with managing as many as nine funds, including rebalancing, and have the minimum funds that warrant doing so (an arbitrary minimum would be $100,000), you should seriously consider the SuperSmart Portfolio. The long-term data on tilting your portfolio toward small and value stocks is solid. While not predictive, it is likely that investors will continue to be rewarded in the future (over the long term) for taking on this additional risk.

This portfolio is especially appealing for investors who can take more stock market risk. It makes sense that the SuperSmart Portfolio would excel when the stock portion of a portfolio increases, because the overweighting of small and value stocks affects only the stock allocation.

At the more aggressive levels of risk, the difference in returns is meaningful. For example, for the 20-year historical return period, the SuperSmart Portfolio outperformed the Smartest Index Fund Portfolio by 1.2% annually at the medium-high-risk level (80% stocks, 20% bonds) and by 2.06% at the high-risk level (100% stocks). A $10,000 investment, at the medium-high-risk level, over the 20-year period, would have increased in value to $65,201 for the SuperSmart Portfolio compared to only $52,167 for the Smartest Index Fund Portfolio.

In the high-risk category, the numbers are even more compelling. The SuperSmart Portfolio had an ending value of $76,651 compared to an ending value of only $52,649 for the Smartest Index Fund Portfolio.

There's a reason why it's SuperSmart.

If this portfolio is not feasible for you, the Smartest Index Fund Portfolio was a very close runner-up. It has the advantage of having only three funds, which makes investing and rebalancing very easy. The fact that you can control the allocation between U.S. and international stocks is a definite plus. However, it does not have exposure to international bonds.

This portfolio is especially appealing for investors with a smaller allocation to stocks and a larger allocation to bonds. In the 20-year low-risk category (20% stocks, 80% bonds) and medium-low-risk category (40% stocks, 60% bonds), it outperformed the SuperSmart Portfolio. Its returns in the medium-risk level (60% stocks, 40% bonds) were only very marginally (0.39%) lower.

While the Smartest ETF Portfolio came in last, it is still worthy of consideration. It has an international bond component, which may improve its future performance, depending on the returns of that asset class compared to U.S. bonds. Its allocation to international stocks may be too high for some investors, but that allocation may pay off if these stocks enjoy superior returns, compared to U.S. stocks. It has only three funds, so it is easy to purchase and rebalance.

What's the Point?

The historical returns of the SuperSmart Portfolio validate the research of Fama and French, especially for investors who can take significant stock market risk, but both of the other Smartest Portfolios offer benefits worthy of serious consideration.

PART FIVE

Going It Alone
or Getting Advice

Investing on your own, without a broker or adviser, makes sense for some investors but not for others. There are a number of key issues to resolve in order to make the decision that is best for you.

CHAPTER 27

Asking the Wrong Question

Sometimes you have to learn how to give the right answer to the wrong *question*.
—Warren Minor Christopher, American diplomat and lawyer

When it comes to investing on your own or with a broker or adviser, the real issue is often lost in the polarizing discourse. On the one side are the advisers and brokers who believe every investor benefits from their services. On the other side are those investors who do not believe the fees and service justify retaining them.

I believe both sides are asking the wrong question. The question is not, Should you use a broker or adviser? It's far more complicated and requires consideration of the following factors:

- If you are a small investor (under $100,000), the issue may be moot, since many brokers and advisers will not take accounts below certain minimums or may charge you fees if your account falls below these levels. Even if you can find someone who is willing to take your account, it may not be worth the additional fees. For example, if you were to select the Smartest Target Date Portfolio, it basically is "set it and forget it." You don't need any assistance to implement it.

- The wrong adviser will be wrong for you, regardless of the size of your portfolio. If your broker engages in active management and attempts to beat the markets by investing in actively managed mutual funds, picking stocks, or timing the market, you are likely to be harmed by this advice. It's one thing to decide you need assistance. It's another to use a broker who transfers your wealth to his or her pocket.

- If you intend to invest on your own as an *active* investor, consider the fact that the average active fund investor lost money over the past 20 years, after inflation and taxes. It's only when you are committed to capturing the returns of the global market for the stock *and* bond portions of your portfolio that you should even consider investing on your own. Even then, there are strong data indicating that paying for an adviser who recommends capturing global returns using index or passively managed funds is not simply a cost to you but an investment that can yield significant returns.

- Do you have the time and enjoy managing your money? Some people like to take total control of their investing. You now have enough information so that you can purchase a very sophisticated, risk-adjusted portfolio. If this is something you enjoy and have the time to do, you could consider going it alone, but you should be aware of data indicating that you might be better off with a passive adviser.

- Do you have admirable personal discipline? There's a saying among competitive athletes that "it's easy to be a good winner." It's also easy to have discipline in a bull market. A bear market is quite another story. When the market tanked in 2008 and the early part of 2009, many investors panicked and fled to safety.

They missed out on the subsequent recovery. If you had a competent adviser—or were following the Smart Investing advice—you were already in the right asset allocation and made no changes. And your adviser may have guided you to rebalance by purchasing asset classes that were hemorrhaging losses. Few individual investors without advisers had the courage to do both.

- Do you understand the impact of fees on returns? Everyone agrees that low fees correlate with higher returns. But what about the fees charged by advisers? Unless your adviser can justify his or her fees by demonstrating returns superior to what you can achieve on your own or by adding value in other ways, you need to consider these fees, just as you would consider all other fees. The Smartest Portfolios use only low management fee index funds. These funds keep the fees you pay to an absolute minimum.

- Do you refuse to pay for investment advice? One survey found that approximately 54.5 million Americans (47% of all U.S. households) own stocks or bonds. Approximately two thirds of these investors consulted with a financial adviser during the five years preceding the survey. That means that approximately 18 million investors did not use any broker or adviser. The survey found that 82% of investors younger than 40 used the Internet for a financial-related purpose. Also, 74% of those between 40 and 64 used the Internet, and 47% of those age 65 or higher did so. For many investors, the Internet has either augmented the services received from brokers and advisers or replaced them altogether. You may have decided that the Internet gives you all the information you need. Or you may have lost so much faith in the securities industry that you refuse to pay *any* adviser for money management services. For whatever reason, there are millions just like you. If you have decided—for good, bad, or no reason—

not to retain an adviser, you should still be able to have the best portfolio available. You now have the information that permits you to do so.

Investing is not rocket science. Smart Investing is actually quite simple and straightforward, once you understand the fundamentals. Basic principles of asset allocation, global diversification using low management fee index funds, and rebalancing are easy to understand and simple to implement. I have given you four Smartest Portfolios, including a very sophisticated one in the SuperSmart Portfolio, that you can manage on your own. Implementing any of these portfolios should permit you to capture returns over the long term significantly in excess of those attained by many investment professionals. Nevertheless, there is another side to this story, which you should carefully consider before making this important decision.

Investing is like doing your taxes: If you have a very straightforward return, you can probably file it on your own or with the help of an online tax program. But if your filings are more complicated, you should find yourself a competent professional who can handle a wide range of tax situations. If you fall into the following categories, you probably need an adviser:

- You are the trustee of a trust with assets to invest, or the sponsor of a retirement plan (like a 401[k] plan). Your conduct as trustee may be regulated by the Uniform Prudent Investor Act (UPIA), which governs the conduct of investment fiduciaries. This act has been adopted in 44 states and the District of Columbia, and other states have adopted part of the act. The UPIA requires the kind of sophisticated risk-return analysis incorporated into the Smartest Portfolios as a guide to investment decisions by trustees. It permits a trustee to delegate investment decisions to qualified and supervised advisers. Trustees who do so (provided they select a qualified and appropriate adviser) can protect themselves from liability.

- Your conduct as a plan administer is governed by the Employee Retirement Income Security Act (ERISA), which places serious legal responsibility on plan administrators to act solely in the best interest of plan participants. Retaining the right adviser, who is what is known as a "3(38) ERISA fiduciary," can transfer 100% of the liability for the selection and monitoring of investment options in the plan from you to them.

- You have no interest in finance and would like to spend your time on activities you enjoy.

- You want continuity with your investments for your spouse and family when you die.

- You need help with asset allocation and ongoing guidance with rebalancing and, where appropriate, tax loss harvesting, a process by which securities are sold at a loss that is used to offset future capital gains tax liability.

- You know yourself and understand you don't have the discipline to stay the course when the going gets tough in the markets.

- You are a serious student of the capital markets. You have studied the data and believe funds managed by Dimensional Fund Advisors (DFA) (available only through authorized advisers), in an appropriate risk-adjusted portfolio, offer superior returns to those you can obtain on your own, net of adviser's fees, even using the Smartest Portfolios. (For a discussion of Dimensional funds, see Chapter 31.)

If you fit into any of these categories, you need an adviser. You are in good company. There are 36 million households who rely on advisers for investing guidance. Unfortunately, most of them have chosen the wrong adviser and have paid the price.

I discuss the qualifications of the right adviser in the next chapter.

What's the Point?

Doing it yourself is a viable option for some investors but not for others.

CHAPTER 28

Fooling the Fans, but Not the Players

A fool despises good counsel, but a wise man takes it to heart.
—Confucius

An odd dance takes place when investment advisers write books about investing. The books are filled with a dizzying amount of impressive data, designed to convey to the reader that the author really knows his or her stuff. Near the end of these books is usually a chapter called "How to Pick an Investment Adviser." The author describes the ideal background and experience of an adviser. By the remotest of coincidence, when you check out the biography of the author, he or she fits the bill down to the last detail. Maybe some of the fans (readers) are fooled, but the players (other advisers) are not.

For those of you who do not want to use an adviser, I have shown you exactly how to invest on your own. For those of you who are still considering an adviser, I am about to give you my how-to-choose-an-adviser advice, but at least I gave you fair warning! I can also tell you that, while most advisers will not meet all of these qualifications, there are many who do. It's worth your time to find them.

I have known terrible advisers with impressive credentials and great advisers with modest credentials. When choosing an adviser, your primary focus should be on his or her investment philosophy.

Your adviser should:

- Focus on your asset allocation, and recommend a globally diversified, risk-adjusted portfolio consisting *solely* of low management fee, passively managed funds, index funds, or exchange-traded funds.

- Charge on a fully disclosed and transparent fee basis and should not receive any other compensation.

- Have the ability to monitor your accounts and provide timely and accurate reports to you.

- Be able to rebalance your accounts in a timely and tax-efficient manner.

- Have the experience and know-how to engage in tax loss harvesting where appropriate and alert you to tax loss harvesting opportunities.

- Be skilled in the use of tax-managed funds in your taxable accounts.

- Publish the portfolios he or she recommends (at various risk levels) and provide extensive, long-term risk and return data for those portfolios (as has been provided for the Smartest Portfolios in this book).

- Not accept funds directly from you. He or she should use a well-known, independent custodian (like Charles Schwab, Fidelity Investments, or TD Ameritrade). Accounts should be opened in your name directly with that custodian. Funds should be wired directly into that account. Checks should be made out to the order of the custodian for deposit in your account and never to the adviser. You should be able to access your account 24/7 on the website of the custodian. If you follow these basic steps, you will "Madoff-proof" your money.

- Have a competent back office, consisting of analysts who can review and assess portfolios and 401(k) plans. You will be surprised at how frequently you will need this kind of analysis done.

- Have an experienced trading department and insurance to cover trading errors. Major custodians have an entire department devoted to dealing with trading errors. They are very common and can be costly. Be sure your adviser will stand behind the trades placed on your behalf. A professional adviser should have trade error and liability insurance and fidelity bonding for all employees and should be willing to show you proof of this insurance.

- Provide necessary service after the sale. I am amazed at the amount of work required to properly service the needs of investment clients. Typical requests include deposits and withdrawals, ensuring that all accounts are properly titled, setting up new accounts, dealing with conversions to Roth plans (including doing the required analysis), opening accounts for individual IRA plans, and dealing with divorce issues and transfers on death. It's critical for you to be able to reach your adviser, or the administrative staff, promptly. All of your requests should be taken care of efficiently and to your complete satisfaction.

- Have a well-staffed compliance department and be fully compliant. Compliance is a huge issue and cost for advisers. You don't want an adviser whose business has been censured or may be shut down by the regulatory authorities. Ask to see copies of recent audit reports. Satisfy yourself that there are no regulatory issues that could affect the continued operations of your adviser. One easy way to do this is to review Form ADV, Uniform Application for Investment Advisor Registration, on file with the Securities and Exchange Commission (SEC). Item 11 requires disclosure on disciplinary history. You can review these reports on the SEC's website (http://adviserinfo.sec.gov/%28S%28t5lli045pcyb5n45ffvtc 045%29%29/IAPD/Content/Search/iapd_Search.aspx).

Finally, I know this seems obvious, but it is often overlooked by investors: *Visit the office of the adviser.* You will learn a lot from that experience. Many discount advisers do not have an office or support staff. This should be a red flag. You will be entrusting your life savings to your adviser. It's worth a trip to see what kind of an operation he or she is running. "Cheap" can turn out to be very expensive.

What's the Point?

There are many factors that should determine your choice of an adviser. Your adviser's investment philosophy is the right place to start.

CHAPTER 29

An Unlikely Source of Returns

No tears in the writer, no tears in the reader. No surprise in the writer, no surprise in the reader.

—Robert Frost

This fact may surprise you: Your adviser should not be just an expense, but a source of returns that makes the fee you pay an investment. Numerous studies have shown that index investors have historically outperformed the average fund investor. What's more revealing is how the performance of index investors *with* advisers compares to index investors *without* advisers.

Studies published in the *Morningstar Indexes Yearbook* for 2005 and *The Little Book of Common Sense Investing,* by John Bogle, calculated the percentage of reported fund returns obtained by these two categories of investors and found that index investors *without* passive advisers captured from 78% to 88% of fund returns. Why not 100% (or more) of the returns? Buffeted by the winds of turbulent markets, investors without the guidance of passive advisers bounced in and out of the markets, usually at the wrong time.

Another study also published in the *Morningstar Indexes Yearbook* showed that investors in passive funds (index funds) managed by

DFA captured 109% of the reported returns of their funds. These investors were able to capture more than 100% of the reported returns of their DFA funds because their advisers not only kept them invested but also had a disciplined program of rebalancing. The study explained these stellar returns by noting that "advisors who use DFA encourage very smart behavior among their clients, even buying more out-of-favor segments of the market and riding them up, rather than buying at the peak and riding the trend down, which is usually the case with fund investors."

Index fund investors with or without advisers did markedly better than fund investors who were in actively managed funds. These investors captured anywhere from 15% to 73% of fund returns, depending on the time period measured and whether the funds were stock or bond funds. The returns for bond investors were at the lower end of the range.

I recently had an experience with a client who was very focused on fees. He compared our fees with those of another adviser—and our fees were higher. He showed me the portfolio recommended by the other adviser. I pointed out that a micro cap fund recommended by the other adviser did have higher returns than the comparable fund we were recommending, but the tax impact was greater than our fund. When I compared the after-tax returns of the two funds, our fund saved him $10,000 a year. I also ran an analysis showing how critical it was to maintain his risk profile. It indicated that even a minor deviation would more than wipe out the difference in fees.

Don't get me wrong. Fees, including adviser fees, are critically important. However, they are only part of the overall picture. You want to consider total return and after-tax returns (both net of an adviser's fees) as well. As was the case with this client, the adviser with the higher fee may turn out to be a better option when all factors are evaluated.

You should understand there are hard data indicating the fee you pay the *right* adviser can be (but is not always) a source of returns.

What's the Point?

Fees paid to advisers make sense if they're an investment and not just an expense.

CHAPTER 30

Don't Confuse Knowledge with Success

An amazing thing, the human brain. Capable of understanding incredibly complex and intricate concepts. Yet at times unable to recognize the obvious and simple.

—Jay Abraham, marketing consultant

You now have the knowledge to be a very sophisticated investor. Don't confuse that knowledge with automatic success. Knowledge is the easy part. The discipline to stay invested when the markets tank eludes most investors. They typically jump in and out of the markets at wrong times.

The recent turbulence in the markets is an excellent example of this conduct. Consider this timeline:

October 9, 2007: The Dow Jones Industrial Average (DJIA) reached an all-time high of 14,164.

March 9, 2009: The DJIA reached the bottom of the ensuing bear market, closing at 6,507.

March 31, 2011: The DJIA closed at 12,319, marking an extraordinary recovery.

A knowledgeable and disciplined investor would have stayed the course throughout this turbulent period. But that's not what most investors did. In October 2009, net inflows to bond funds and out of equities peaked at $231 billion. These investors missed out on the huge run-up of stocks, which continued into 2011.

A competent adviser understands long-term data and insists that his or her clients fully appreciate the potential for short-term volatility when they decide on their initial asset allocation. There's a quantifiable advantage to having an adviser who provides this perspective.

Tax Loss Harvesting

A knowledgeable adviser can add value by engaging in tax loss harvesting where appropriate, which can have a significant impact on funds that are invested outside of qualified plans. Tax loss harvesting lets you sell funds in your taxable accounts that have losses, simultaneously purchase a different fund with the same benchmark, and repurchase the original funds 31 days or more from the sale of the original funds.

Harvesting these losses has meaningful tax advantages: You can apply $3,000 of your net capital losses annually to offset your ordinary income. The balance of your capital losses can be carried over and offset against short- or long-term capital gains (depending on the type of capital loss you incurred) in the future, until it is used up.

There is no reason why you can't discipline yourself to follow the long-term data and stay invested and to engage in tax loss harvesting, when appropriate. The reality is that most investors think they can, but often they don't. Competent advisers will be checking the portfolios of their clients and alerting them to tax loss harvesting opportunities. Few investors will do this on their own.

Finally, the right adviser can be a source of ongoing trustworthy advice and support, when you feel buffeted by all the financial news telling you to get in or out of the markets. I have a client who is conservatively invested. He is convinced the markets will continue their recovery in 2011 and beyond. He wanted to change his asset allocation from 60% stocks and 40% bonds to 100% stocks. I reviewed the long-term data with him with some very telling results.

In 2008, his portfolio lost 23% of its value (which he recovered in 2009–2010). Over the last 50 years, the average of annualized returns for an investor who held a similar portfolio for any 8-year rolling monthly period was 10.46%. A portfolio with 100% stocks lost 41% of its value in 2008. Over the last 50 years, the average of annualized returns for an investor who held that portfolio for any 15-year rolling monthly period was 13.57%.

The questions raised by this analysis were the following:

1. Was he prepared to hold the more aggressive portfolio for a minimum of 15 years before withdrawing 20% or more of it?

2. Were the additional returns worth the greater volatility?

3. Did he appreciate the possibility of a black swan event, which could make the downside significantly worse?

He was prepared to hold the portfolio for a minimum of 15 years but answered no to the next two questions. He decided to stay with the more conservative portfolio. Many investors need an adviser who can provide that kind of analysis and perspective.

What's the Point?

Personal discipline and tax loss harvesting are two issues to consider when deciding whether to use an adviser.

CHAPTER 31

The Dimensional Difference

Consistent with Fama's theories, Dimensional Fund Advisors is
agnostic about which stocks it buys. Its fund managers do little or
no company research. They don't schmooze with chief executives
or dial in to earnings conference calls.
—Seth Lubove, financial journalist

No book about "smart portfolios" would be complete without discussing Dimensional Fund Advisors (DFA).

DFA believes that investing is a "financial science." Its goal is to "deliver the performance of capital markets and increase returns through state-of-the-art portfolio design and trading." Its core belief is that capital markets are efficient and efforts to "beat the markets" are likely to be futile. DFA does not engage in stock picking or market timing. Instead, it focuses on these five dimensions of risk: (1) exposure to the stock market, (2) amount of small company stocks, (3) amount of value company stocks, (4) term risk, and (5) default risk. Exposure to small and value stocks is applicable to its stock funds. Term and default risk is applicable to its bond funds.

Eugene Fama and Kenneth French are board members of DFA. Other noted academics are also affiliated with it.

DFA does not use standard indexes (like those used by Vanguard and most ETFs) as benchmarks for its funds. It designs its indexes to capture the risk factors it believes account for almost all returns. As you might expect, DFA strictly adheres to the Fama-French three-factor model.

With $206 billion currently under management, DFA's list of clients includes high net worth individuals, public funds, major corporations, Taft-Hartley Funds, and nonprofit organizations. Individual investors can only access funds managed by DFA through authorized financial advisers. In the United States, there are a small number of advisers who have gone through the training and been approved by DFA to do so.

These advisers (I am one of them) receive no compensation from DFA (or any other incentive) for placing their clients' assets with them. Nor are the advisers required to designate DFA as the sole fund manager for their clients' assets.

There is a heated debate among financial experts about whether DFA's passively managed funds, Vanguard's index funds, or a portfolio of ETFs is the best choice for investors. There is also much discussion among investors and the investing community about the value of a financial adviser. Much of the argument misses the real point.

The two critical decisions you need to make are these:

Will you be active or passively invested?

Will you benefit from an adviser to implement your chosen investment strategy?

The SuperSmart Portfolio and a portfolio of DFA funds both have the benefit of a tilt toward small size and value companies, which will give you higher returns when those asset classes outperform. A portfolio of DFA funds comes with the cost of an advisory fee but, as explained previously, DFA investors historically have more than made up for these fees by capturing significantly greater market returns.

Efforts to study the returns of DFA's funds and compare them to those of Vanguard and ETFs have been inconclusive. In one study, Edward Tower, a professor at Duke University, and Cheng-Ying Yang, a PhD candidate in economics at the University of Wisconsin, compared data on funds managed by DFA and Vanguard from 1999 to 2006. They found significant outperformance by DFA during this limited period. However, a subsequent study by Professor Tower over the 10-year period from 1998 to 2008 was unable to duplicate those findings. Professor Tower concluded that he was unable to rank the performance of DFA against Vanguard and ETFs.

What's the Point?

DFA versus Vanguard and ETFs is an important debate, but the real issue is active versus passive management.

CHAPTER 32

The Takeaway

Nobody can go back and start a new beginning, but anyone can start
today and make a new ending.
—Maria Robinson, author

I t's time for a new ending.

I have seen up close and personal the impact of poor investing
advice. We have an entire system of investing designed to transfer
wealth from those who have it to those who manage it, which can
destroy lives and ruin dreams.

Smart Investing is not complicated. Relying on brokers or advisers
who claim to be able to predict the future is simply foolish. It's time for
you to fundamentally change in the way you invest.

Follow these rules. They will put you in charge of your financial
life:

1. If you are using a broker or adviser who claims to be able to beat
   the market, withdraw your money and close your account.

2. Don't own any individual stocks or bonds. One exception for
   bonds might be for extremely wealthy investors who can purchase enough bonds to diversify their risk and are prepared to

hold the bonds in what is called a laddered bond portfolio, which consists of bonds with different maturities and is used to provide a steady stream of income and to moderate interest rate fluctuations. It is typically held to maturity. Even in this exceptional case, extraordinary care must be taken in the selection of a broker or adviser who will provide—in writing—the criteria governing the selection of bonds for your portfolio.

3. Ignore stock market pundits who make predictions about the direction of the markets and price movement of stocks. They are not psychic.

4. Determine your asset allocation and invest in a globally diversified portfolio of low management fee stock and bond *index* funds. Never deviate from this basic approach to investing.

5. Avoid overweighting your portfolio in fad investments of all kinds, including gold.

6. There is no relationship between the amount of research you do about a particular stock and the returns you are likely to receive if you buy or sell it.

7. Excellent companies do not make excellent investments.

8. Neither you nor your broker nor your adviser is smarter than the millions of people looking at the publicly available information about a particular stock and setting a price for that stock. The price they set is likely to be a fair price. Investing based on any other assumption is gambling. The expected return on gambling is zero (or less because of high transaction costs).

9. You should be rewarded for each unit of risk you take. When confronted with two portfolios with the same expected return, select the one with the least amount of risk.

10. If you don't know the risk of your investments, you have no business investing.

11. Focus on the after-tax return of your investments. Pre-tax returns can be very misleading, particularly with actively managed stock funds.

12. Accept the reality that Eugene Fama and Kenneth French know more about investing than you do. If you can handle the Super-Smart Portfolio, which is based on their three-factor model, you should consider it, especially if your tolerance for risk permits significant exposure to stocks.

13. Any one of the Smartest Portfolios recommended in this book is a far better option than a portfolio that is actively managed.

14. Don't reject retaining an adviser based solely on fees. DFA investors have historically captured more return than active investors and even index investors without advisers. Consider the totality of the data, which includes historical returns.

15. The single most important decision you can make is to renounce active management. Investing should be based on data and not on the musings and self-interest of "experts" who lack both the expertise they purport to have and any accountability for their advice.

What's the Point?

You have the power—and now you have the tools—to be a smart, responsible investor.

CHAPTER 33

Says Who?

Truth stands, even if there be no public support. It is self-sustained.
—Mohandas Gandhi

There's an anomaly when it comes to investing. The way most individuals invest is supported by precious little data. "Data" are rarely mentioned by a majority of brokers. How often has your broker supported his or her advice by sending you a peer-reviewed study that appeared in a financial journal, or given you long-term risk and return data?

Would you trust a doctor who prescribed medication that was not supported by published, reliable research? Of course not. Yet most investors base their investment decisions on casual statements made by self-proclaimed investment professionals, or pundits appearing on television, with nothing more than their opinions to back up the advice they so freely (and confidently) dispense.

The Smartest Portfolios are supported by reams of data. You need the comfort of knowing there is a sound basis for investing the right way. When sources are available online, the URL is provided to the source. To make it easier for you to access these websites, you can find hyperlinks to all of the sources at www.smartestinvestment book.com.

Introduction: A Lesson from Einstein

I highly recommend the following books:

Bernstein, William, *The Intelligent Asset Allocator*, McGraw-Hill Professional: New York, 2000.

Bogle, John C., *The Little Book of Common Sense Investing*, Wiley: Hoboken, NJ, 2007.

Hebner, Mark T., *Index Funds: The 12-Step Program for Active Investors*, Index Funds Advisors: Irvine, CA, 2006, p. 392.

Larimore, Taylor, Mel Lindauer, and Michael LeBoeuf, *The Boglehead's Guide to Investing*, Wiley: Hoboken, NJ, 2007.

Malkiel, Burton G., *A Random Walk Down Wall Street*, Norton: New York, 1973.

You can read a very informative and entertaining piece on the merits of active versus passive management by Rex Sinquefield, cofounder of Dimensional Fund Advisors. His opening statement in a debate with Donald Yacktman at the Schwab Institutional conference in San Francisco, October 12, 1995, can be found on this website: www.dfaus .com/2009/05/active-vs-passive-management.html.

A video of an interview with Sinquefield can be viewed on the Index Fund Advisors' website: www.ifa.com/advisorcam.

1. A Battle for Your Brain

Jason Zweig is the author of *Your Money and Your Brain: How the New Science of Neuroeconomics Can Help Make You Rich* (Simon & Schuster: New York, 2007). He is also a personal finance columnist for the *Wall Street Journal*. The quote is from Jason Zweig, "Brain Tour: It's a Pleasure," CNN Money, September 27, 2002. Available at http://money .cnn.com/2002/09/16/pf/investing/agenda_brain5/index.htm.

View brain images showing the flare-up of "nucleus accumbens" of investors and addicts on the Index Fund Advisors' website: www.ifa .com/12steps/step1/step1page2.asp#brain.

Zweig explained the effect of the dopamine rush in his article "Brain Tour: It's a Pleasure," CNN Money, September 27, 2002. Available at http:// money.cnn.com/2002/09/16/pf/investing/agenda_brain5/index.htm.

Find more information about the study involving two videos of the same lecturer on *The Psy-Fi Blog*, "The Halo Effect: What's in a Company Name?," July 9, 2009. Available at www.psyfitec.com/2009/07/ halo-effect-whats-in-company-name.html.

The study about the effect of changing the name of a mutual fund is Michael J. Cooper, Huseyin Gulen, and Raghavendra Rau, "Changing Names with Style: Mutual Fund Name Changes and Their Effects on Fund Flows," paper no. 293, presented at the EFA 2003 Annual Conference, Glasgow, Scotland, August 2003. Available at http://papers.ssrn .com/sol3/papers.cfm?abstract_id=423989.

2. In Bizarro World, These Traits Would Be Valued

For further details about the junk bond scandal, see the article "Michael Milken" on Wikipedia: www.en.wikipedia.org/wiki/Michael_ Milken#Scandal.

For a discussion of the emails sent by analysts, see David Teather, "The Whores of Wall Street," *Guardian*, October 2, 2002. Available at www.guardian.co.uk/business/2002/oct/02/usnews.international news.

For details of the settlement of the analyst fraud scandal and the names of the settling defendants, see "Regulators Announce $1.4 Billion Settlement with Wall Street," *USA Today*, December 20, 2002 (updated March 27, 2003). Available at www.usatoday.com/money/ companies/regulation/2002-12-19-settlement-usat_x.htm.

For a discussion of the Janus excessive trading settlement, see Christine Dugas and John Waggoner, "Janus to Pay $225M to Settle

Charges," *USA Today*, April 27, 2004. Available at www.usatoday.com/money/perfi/funds/2004-04-27-janus-settlement_x.htm.

The press release announcing the Bear Stearns late trading settlement can be found at the SEC's website: "SEC Settles Fraud Charges with Bear Stearns for Late Trading and Market Timing Violations," March 16, 2006. Available at www.sec.gov/news/press/2006-38.htm.

For details of the Bank of America settlement, see Otis Bilodeau, "Bank of America Fined $26 Million for Research Abuse," Bloomberg .com, March 14, 2007. Available at www.bloomberg.com/apps/news?pid=newsarchive&sid=agWFohbjP_6U&refer=home.

For an insightful article on the subprime mortgage crisis, see John Cassidy, "Scandals," *New Yorker*, May 3, 2010. Available at www.newyorker.com/talk/comment/2010/05/03/100503taco_talk_cassidy.

The machinations of Merrill Lynch relating to subprime mortgages are described in Jake Bernstein and Jesse Eisinger, "The 'Subsidy': How a Handful of Merrill Lynch Bankers Helped Blow Up Their Own Firm," *ProPublica*, December 22, 2010. Available at www.propublica .org/article/the-subsidy-how-merrill-lynch-traders-helped-blow-up-their-own-firm.

Senator Levin's report alleges that Goldman Sachs misled Congress when it testified about profiting from collaterized debt obligations. He recommended that federal prosecutors determine whether perjury charges should be brought against officers of the firm who gave this testimony. See "Goldman Sachs Misled Congress, Duped Clients, Levin Says," *Bloomberg Businessweek*, April 14, 2011. Available at www.businessweek.com/news/2011-04-14/goldman-sachs-misled-congress-duped-clients-levin-says.html. Goldman Sachs has denied these charges. You can find a complete copy of the report at www.ft.com/cms/fc7d55c8-661a-11e0-9d40-00144feab49a.pdf.

Lehman's fall from grace and the desperate efforts of Merrill Lynch to survive are set forth by Andrew Ross Sorkin, "Lehman Files for

Bankruptcy; Merrill Is Sold," *New York Times*, September 14, 2008. Available at www.nytimes.com/2008/09/15/business/15lehman.html. The restructuring of the major players in the financial services industry is described by Stephen Labaton, "Agency's '04 Rule Let Banks Pile Up New Debt," *New York Times*, October 2, 2008. Available at www.nytimes.com/2008/10/03/business/03sec.html?_r=1.

The SEC press release concerning credit rating agencies can be found on its website: "SEC Approves Measures to Strengthen Oversight of Credit Rating Agencies," December 3, 2008. Available at www .sec.gov/news/press/2008/2008-284.htm.

In a study done by the Federal Reserve Board in December 2003, the authors correctly noted: "Bond rating agencies have an obvious conflict of interest. They have a financial incentive to accommodate the preferences of bond issuers because they are selected and paid by the issuers." Inexplicably, the study concluded that this conflict did not affect the integrity of the ratings. See Daniel M. Covitz and Paul Harrison, "Testing Conflicts of Interest at Bond Ratings Agencies with Market Anticipation: Evidence That Reputation Incentives Dominate," Federal Reserve Board, Washington, DC, 2003. Available at www.federal reserve.gov/pubs/feds/2003/200368/200368pap.pdf.

Details of Bank of America's recent settlement relating to buyers of municipal bond derivatives can be found at "BofA Pays $137 Million to Settle Fraud Charges," CNBC.com, December 7, 2010. Available at www.cnbc.com/id/40551830.

3. Investing Without Eddie O'Neal

For details of the internal report, which should have placed Banco Santander on notice about Madoff, see James Quinn, "Santander Suspicious of Bernard Madoff in 2006," *Telegraph*, May 19, 2010. Available at www.telegraph.co.uk/finance/financetopics/bernard-madoff/ 7741884/Santander-suspicious-of-Bernard-Madoff-in-2006.html.

For a chilling account of the obvious red flags in Madoff's operation and the failure of the SEC to act even when it had compelling information about his Ponzi scheme, I highly recommend Harry Markopolos, *No One Would Listen: A True Financial Thriller* (Wiley: Hoboken, NJ, 2011).

The thin credentials of Madoff's auditors are described by Alyssa Abkowitz, "Madoff's Auditor . . . Doesn't Audit?" CNN Money, December 19, 2008. Available at www.money.cnn.com/2008/12/17/news/com panies/madoff.auditor.fortune/index.htm.

For a list of feeder funds for Madoff, see "UK: SFO Investigating Madoff Feeder Funds," Securities Docket, March 30, 2009. Available at www.securitiesdocket.com/2009/03/30/uk-sfo-investigating-madoff-feeder-funds.

See also Simon Bowers, "Serious Fraud Office Broadens Investigation to Madoff Feeders," *Guardian*, March 27, 2009. Available at www .guardian.co.uk/business/2009/mar/27/serious-fraud-office-bernard -madoff-feeder-funds.

For details of the Madoff-related fees generated by the feeder funds, see Tom Lauricella, "Feeder Fees Topped $790 Million," *Wall Street Journal*. April 11, 2009. Available at http://online.wsj.com/article/SB1239 40737747310069.html.

For a discussion of how Fairfield Sentry failed to spot the Madoff red flags, see Alex Berenson and Eric Konigsberg, "Firm Built on Madoff Ties Faces Tough Questions," *New York Times*, December 21, 2008. Available at www.nytimes.com/2008/12/22/business/22fairfield .html?pagewanted=1&_r=1.

4. Join a Wise Crowd

The referenced study on the performance of investment clubs is Brad M. Barber and Terrance Odean, "Too Many Cooks Spoil the Profits: The Performance of Investment Clubs." Available at http://faculty .haas.berkeley.edu/odean/papers/clubs/Clubs_4-99.pdf.

The wisdom of crowds is not universally accepted. Daniel Tammet, *Embracing the Wide Sky* (Free Press: New York, 2009) cites the example of an online chess match between chess master Gary Kasparov and tens of thousands of online chess players. Kasparov prevailed. However, this crowd would not be deemed "wise" based on the criteria set forth by Surowiecki.

5. Trading Against Goldman Sachs

For a discussion of the contribution of trading for their own account on the profits of major Wall Street firms, see John Cassidy, "What Good Is Wall Street?" *New Yorker*, November 29, 2010. Available at www .newyorker.com/reporting/2010/11/29/101129fa_fact_cassidy?current Page=all.

So-called proprietary trading will be forbidden by financial reform legislation passed by Congress.

For a discussion of the profits generated by Goldman Sachs from its trading activities, see the company's press release dated October 19, 2010, at www.goldmansachs.com/our-firm/press/press-releases/archived/2010/pdfs/2010-q3-earnings.pdf.

6. What You Can *Really* Learn from Dr. Doom

The website for Roubini Global Economics is www.roubini.com.

Roubini was extolled as a market visionary. See Katie Benner and Christopher Tkaczyk, "8 Who Saw the Crisis Coming," *Fortune*, August 2008. Available at www.money.cnn.com/galleries/2008/fortune/0808/gallery.whosawitcoming.fortune/index.html.

The evolution of Roubini from an obscure professor of economics to Dr. Doom is set forth in this article by Stephen Mihm, "Dr. Doom," *New York Times*, August 15, 2008. Available at www.nytimes.com/2008/08/17/magazine/17pessimist-t.html. The article notes that, as a result of his accurate prediction of the housing crisis, "Roubini, a respected but formerly obscure academic, has become a major figure in the public debate about the economy: the seer who saw it coming. He has been summoned to speak before Congress, the Council on Foreign Relations and the World Economic Forum at Davos. He is now a sought-after advisor, spending much of his time shuttling between meetings with central bank governors and finance ministers in Europe and Asia."

Roubini seemed to believe in his predictive powers. See Beth Kowitt, Jon Birger, and Brian O'Keefe, "8 Really, *Really* Scary Predictions," *Fortune*, December 2008. Available at www.money.cnn.com/galleries/2008/fortune/0812/gallery.market_gurus.fortune/index.html.

David Lereah's prediction about housing prices got him on a top 10 list no one wanted to make. See Morgan Housel, "The Top 10 Worst Predictions of the Financial Crisis," *The Motley Fool*, November 30, 2010. Available at www.fool.com/investing/general/2010/11/30/the-top-10-worst-predictions-of-the-financial-cris.aspx.

Ben Bernanke's rosy prediction for the U.S. economy is set forth in Ben S. Bernanke, *The Economic Outlook*, testimony given before the Joint Economic Committee, U.S. Congress, March 28, 2007. Available at www.federalreserve.gov/newsevents/testimony/bernanke2007 0328a.htm.

Bernanke tried to defuse his poor prediction with humor. See "Bernanke: About That Housing Crisis Being Contained . . . ," *Wall Street Journal*, July 15, 2008. Available at http://blogs.wsj.com/economics/2008/07/15/bernanke-about-that-housing-crisis-being-contained.

The Laderman study on market timing newsletters is at Jeffrey M. Laderman, "Market Timing: A Perilous Ploy," *Business Week*, March 9, 1998. Available at www.businessweek.com/1998/10/b3568136.htm.

Kiyosaki's reference to the "dead cat bounce" can be found here in Robert Kiyosaki, "2010: The Best of Times or the Worst?," *Yahoo! Finance*, December 29, 2009. Available at www.finance.yahoo.com/expert/article/richricher/211091.

For my calculation concerning the probability of a forecast being correct, I relied on Figure 4-2i on the Index Funds Advisors' website (with whom I am affiliated): www.ifa.com/12steps/step4/step4page2 .asp#ForecastCorrect.

An article in *Business Week* noted that "economists mostly failed to predict the worst economic crisis since the 1930s." Peter Coy, "What Good Are Economists Anyway?," *Bloomberg Businessweek*, April 16, 2009. Available at www.businessweek.com/magazine/content/09_17/ b4128026997269.htm?chan=top+news_economics+subindex+page _economics.

7. The Myth of the Lost Decade

Here are two sources in the financial media that discussed the lost decade:

Farzad, Roben, "A Decade of Decay," *Bloomberg Businessweek*, January 10, 2008. Available at www.businessweek.com/magazine/ content/08_03/b4067071413745.htm.

Gongloff, Mark, "Lost Decade," *Wall Street Journal*, July 3, 2008. Available at http://blogs.wsj.com/marketbeat/2008/07/03/lost-decade.

The video of my (Dan Solin's) confrontation with Jim Cramer can be seen on the *Huffington Post* website at www.huffingtonpost.com/ 2009/04/17/jim-cramer-flips-out-at-h_n_188443.html.

For an excellent summary of why it wasn't a lost decade, see Allan Roth, "Why It Wasn't a Lost Decade for Investors," MoneyWatch, December 18, 2009. Available at www.moneywatch.bnet.com/economic -news/article/why-it-wasnt-a-lost-decade-for-investors/375568/?tag= content;col1.

For a responsible and balanced article debunking the myth of the lost decade, see Ron Lieber, "For Savers, It Was Hardly a Lost Decade,"

New York Times, January 1, 2010. Available at www.nytimes.com/2010/ 01/02/your-money/stocks-and-bonds/02money.html?_r=1.

One study by *Barron's* found that "Cramer's recommendations underperform the market by most measures." See Bill Alpert, "Cramer's Star Outshines His Stock Picks," *Barron's,* February 9, 2009. Available at http://online.barrons.com/article/SB123397107399659271.html#article Tabs_panel_article%3D1.

Another erroneous, common refrain during this period was that "buy and hold is dead," which filled the financial media. See Tom Lydon, "Why Buy-and-Hold Is Dead," ETF Trends, February 10, 2009. Available at www.etftrends.com/2009/02/why-buy-and-hold-is-dead. Lydon noted: "As many know by now, the S&P 500 has done nothing for the last 10 years. It's done less than nothing, in fact."

Lakshman Achuthan, managing director of the Economic Cycle Research Institute, is reported to have declared the classic "buy and hold" strategy for stocks "officially dead." Lakshman Achuthan, "Why 'Buy and Hold' Investing Is Dead and Recessions Are the New Normal," *Huffington Post,* March 29, 2010. Available at www.huffington post.com/2010/03/29/buy-hold-investing-is-dea_n_517788.html.

Retrieve historical prices for the Dow Jones Industrial Average at Yahoo! Finance: www.finance.yahoo.com/q/hp?s=^DJI&a=09&b=9 &c=2007&d=09&e=9&f=2007&g=d.

The source for the portfolio returns from January 1, 2001, through December 31, 2010, is a calculator from Index Funds Advisors (with whom I am affiliated). Available at www.ifa.com/portfolios/ PortReturnCalc/index.aspx. Pay attention to the footnotes to the calculator and the sources and disclosures at the Index Funds Advisors' site.

8. The Myth of the Excellent Company
The investment strategy of one investment advisory firm reflects typical advice: "We want to buy excellent companies and hold them

for the long run." Available at www.bushodonnell.com/investment advisors/analysis.htm.

Find information about *Fortune*'s selection process and the stock returns of the companies who make its list in this article by Matthew Boyle, "Are Good Companies Bad Investments?," *Fortune*, February 26, 2007. Available at www.money.cnn.com/magazines/fortune/fortune_archive/2007/03/05/8401291/index.htm. See also "How We Pick Them," *Fortune* (available at www.money.cnn.com/magazines/fortune/mostadmired/2009/faq) and "World's Most Admired Companies," *Fortune*, March 22, 2010 (available at www.money.cnn.com/magazines/fortune/mostadmired/2010/full_list).

The referenced study on the performance of *Fortune*'s "admired" companies is Meir Statman and Deniz Anginer, "Stocks of Admired Companies and Spurned Ones," SCU Leavey School of Business Research Paper No. 10-02, January 24, 2010. Available at www.ssrn.com/abstract=1540757.

9. The Myth of Holding Individual Stocks

For an excellent discussion on the risk of holding individual stocks, see Craig McCann and Dengpan Luo, "Concentrated Investments, Uncompensated Risk and Hedging Strategies," October 19, 2004. Available at www.slcg.com/documents/Hedging.pdf.

See also Ben McClure, "Modern Portfolio Theory: Why It's Still Hip," Investopedia. Available at www.investopedia.com/articles/06/MPT.asp. McClure correctly notes that "the risk in a portfolio of diverse individual stocks will be less than the risk inherent in holding any one of the individual stocks (provided the risks of the various stocks are not directly related)."

10. The Myth of Holding Individual Bonds

For a discussion of broker markups on bonds, see Alex Anderson, "Broker Markups: A Bond Investor's Worst Enemy," Forbes.com,

February 26, 2009. Available at www.forbes.com/2009/02/26/munis -spreads-markups-personal-finance_investing_ideas_bond_brokers .html.

For a discussion of the impact of bid-ask spreads on bonds and how they affect your costs, see Larry Swedroe, "Ask the Expert," *Moolanomy*, December 3, 2008. Available at www.moolanomy.com/1019/ask -the-expert-with-larry-swedroe-december-2008-issue. Swedroe believes investors with more than $500,000 to invest should consider individual bonds. Other experts strongly disagree. See Scott J. Donaldson, "Taxable Bond Investing: Bond Funds or Individual Bonds," Vanguard Group, March 2005. Available at www.vanguard.com/pdf/taxable bonds.pdf.

11. The Myth of Skill

I published the creation of the Solin Random Stock Index (SRSI) in a blog post dated January 18, 2010: "Can New Index Beat a Chimp's Stock Picks?" Available at www.dailyfinance.com/story/investing/ can-new-index-beat-a-chimps-stock-picks/19319532.

I published the results from January 2010 through November 2010 in a blog post dated December 7, 2010: "New Index Returns Astound Wall Street." Available at www.huffingtonpost.com/dan-solin/new -index-returns-astound_b_792002.html.

This study attributes outperformance by mutual fund managers to luck and not skill: Laurent Barras, O. Scaillet, and Russ R. Wermers, "False Discoveries in Mutual Fund Performance: Measuring Luck in Estimated Alphas," Swiss Finance Institute Research Paper No. 08-18, Robert H. Smith School Research Paper No. RHS 06-043, *Journal of Finance*, April 20, 2009. Available at http://ssrn.com/abstract=869748.

This article discussed the study authored by Laurent Barras, O. Scaillet, and Russ R. Wermers: Mark Hulbert, "The Prescient Are Few," *New York Times*, July 13, 2008. Available at www.nytimes.com/ 2008/07/13/business/13stra.html.

For another study reaching the same conclusion, see Eugene F. Fama and Kenneth R. French, "Luck Versus Skill in the Cross Section of Mutual Fund Returns," Tuck School of Business Working Paper No. 2009-56, Chicago Booth School of Business Research Paper, *Journal of Finance*, December 14, 2009. Available at www.ssrn.com/abstract=1356021.

12. A Potpourri of Other Myths

Conservative political commentator Glenn Beck was criticized for endorsing Goldline International, a precious metals vendor. See Brett Michael Dykes, "Glenn Beck's Gold-Gate Problem," Yahoo! News, December 8, 2010. Available at www.news.yahoo.com/s/ynews/ynews_ts1022.

Gold prices for 200 years can be found at www.onlygold.com.

The lack of predictability about gold prices does not stop pundits from making predictions. In one peer-reviewed study, the authors used a "log-periodic oscillation analysis" to forecast the burst of the gold bubble in April to June 2011. Askar Akaev, Alexey Formin, Sergey V. Tsirel, and Andrewy V. Korotayev, "Log-Periodic Oscillation Analysis Forecasts the Burst of the 'Gold Bubble' in April–June 2011," *Structure and Dynamics* 4 (3) (2010). Available at www.escholarship.org/uc/item/7qk9z9kz.

Information comparing the risk of owning gold to the risk of U.S. Treasury bills can be found at www.ifa.com/emailcampaign/QOW/All_that_Glitters_is_Not_Gold_qow.aspx.

The hedge fund study warning about the risk and return of hedge funds is Burton G. Malkiel and Atanu Saha, "Hedge Funds: Risk and Return," *Financial Analysts Journal* 61 (6) (November/December 2005), pp. 80–88. Available at http://ssrn.com/abstract=872868.

Proponents of hedge funds took issue with this study: George P. Van and Zhiyi Song, "Malkiel-Saha Hedge Fund Paper Flawed," Van HF Advisors International, December 2004. Available at www.intelligenthedgefundinvesting.com/pubs/rb-gvzs.pdf.

This helpful website tracks hedge fund implosions: www.hf-implode.com.

In 2008, despite the market crash, the 25 top hedge fund managers earned an aggregate of $11.6 billion. Louise Story, "Top Hedge Fund Managers Do Well in a Down Year," *New York Times*, March 24, 2009. Available at www.nytimes.com/2009/03/25/business/25hedge.html ?_r=1&ref=business.

Former House Speaker Newt Gingrich is the author of *To Save America: Stopping Obama's Secular-Socialist Machine* (Regnery Press: Washington, DC, 2011).

The cover of *Newsweek* for February 16, 2009, stated: "We Are All Socialists Now." See also Ron Scherer, "Is Obama a Socialist? What Does the Evidence Say?," *Christian Science Monitor*, July 1, 2010. Available at www.csmonitor.com/USA/Politics/2010/0701/Is-Obama-a-socialist-What-does-the-evidence-say.

Typical of the dire prediction for investors as a consequence of the perceived trend toward socialism were these observations by Howard Ruff, of the *Ruff Times*: "It is clear that (President Barack) Obama is an out-of-the-closet socialist, and socialism always leads to inflation. . . . They are creating money by the trillions. As long as they continue to do that, we are going to have inflation." Ruff predicted a multiyear bear market for stocks starting in 2010. He was very wrong. His views were reported in this article: Michael Brush, "10 Pros' Stock Picks for 2010," MSNMoney, December 29, 2009. Available at http://articles.moneycentral.msn.com/Investing/CompanyFocus/10-pros-stock-picks-for-2010.aspx.

The stock returns for socialist countries, compared to the United States, can be found here: "Stock Returns and Socialism," *Trovena*, April 29, 2009. Available at http://blog.trovena.com/2009/04/stock-returns-and-socialism.html?cid=6a00e54fabc18f883401156f695342970c.

The financial media could not report enough on the "new normal." See the following:

Goldstein, Jacob, "An Investment Guru Explains the 'New Normal,'" *Planet Money* (National Public Radio), June 3, 2010. Available at www.npr.org/blogs/money/2010/06/mohamed_elerian_explains _the_n.html.

Hough, Jack, "The New Normal—4% Stock Returns?," Smart-Money, November 20, 2009. Available at www.smartmoney.com/ Investing/Stocks/The-New-Normal-4-Percent-Stock-Returns.

Kimes, Mina, "Investing in the 'New Normal,'" *Fortune*, September 2, 2009. Available at www.money.cnn.com/2009/09/02/pf/funds/ron _muhlenkap_interview.fortune/index.htm.

Nazareth, Rita, and Whitney Kisling, "Old Normal S&P 500 Rally Shows Birinyi Beating Pimco New Normal," Bloomberg.com, November 2, 2010. Available at www.bloomberg.com/news/2010-10-31/old -normal-u-s-stock-rally-shows-birinyi-beating-pimco-new-normal -market.html.

Schurenberg, Eric, "Investing in the 'New Normal,'" MoneyWatch, May 29, 2009. Available at www.moneywatch.bnet.com/retirement -planning/blog/financial-independence/investing-in-the-new -normal/103.

Data showing market returns after a recession is based on a study by Ned Davis Research. Available at www.feuchtfinancial.com/2008 -content/Investing_through_recessions%5B1%5D.pdf.

The lack of correlation between gross domestic product growth and average returns is referenced and discussed in the *IndexUniverse* blog: Larry Swedroe, "Economic Growth and Equity Returns," *Index-Universe*, December 5, 2007. Available at www.indexuniverse.com/sec tions/research/3429-economic-growth-and-equity-returns.html.

The comparison of stock market returns to investors in China and the UK is set forth in the following article: Buttonwood, "The Growth

Illusion," *Economist*, August 28, 2009. The article also references work done by Elroy Dimson, Paul Marsh, and Mike Staunton at the London Business School, who looked at the returns of 17 countries going back to 1900 and found a *negative* correlation between investment returns and growth in GDP per capita. Available at www.economist.com/blogs/buttonwood/2009/08/the_growth_illusion.

For details on the sad saga of holders of Lehman Brothers' Principal Protected Notes, see Zeke Faux and Joshua Gallu, "SEC Said to Review Principal-Protected Note Sales," *Bloomberg Businessweek*, July 2, 2010. Available at www.businessweek.com/news/2010-07-02/sec-said-to-review-principal-protected-note-sales.html.

See also Gretchen Morgenson, " '100% Protected' Isn't as Safe as It Sounds," *New York Times*, May 22, 2010. Available at www.nytimes.com/2010/05/23/business/23gret.html?_r=1.

For a discussion of issues with principal-protected notes, see Duncan Hood, "Protection Racket: Principal-Protected Notes," *MoneySense*, February 2006. Available at www.canadianbusiness.com/my_money/columnists/duncan_hood/article.jsp?content=20060227_115806_4808.

Kenneth R. French (the Care E. and Catherine M. Heidt Professor of Finance at the Tuck School of Business at Dartmouth College) notes the liquidity risk and unnecessary complexity of principal-protected notes in an informative video. Available at www.dimensional.com/famafrench/2010/12/principal-guaranteed-products.html.html?utm_source=feedburner&utm_medium=feed&utm_campaign=Feed%3A+famafrench+(Fama%2FFrench+Forum).

The studies of the returns from an investment in private equity deals are:

Kaplan, Steven N., and Antoinette Schoar, "Private Equity Performance: Returns, Persistence and Capital Flows," MIT Sloan Working Paper No. 4446-03, AFA 2004 San Diego Meetings (November 2003). Available at http://ssrn.com/abstract=473341.

Phalippou, Ludovic, and Oliver Gottschalg, "Performance of Private Equity Funds," paper presented at the EFA 2005 Moscow Meetings. Available at www.ssrn.com/abstract=473221.

The estimate of total investments in private equity deals can be found at "Private Equity," Wikipedia. Available at www.en.wikipedia.org/wiki/Private_equity#Investments_in_private_equity.

13. The Cost of Believing Investing Myths
The following studies discuss the cost of active management:

French, Kenneth R., "The Cost of Active Investing," working paper, April 9, 2008. Available at www.ssrn.com/abstract=1105775.

Miller, Ross M., "Measuring the True Cost of Active Management by Mutual Funds," working paper, June 2005. Available at www.ssrn.com/abstract=746926.

Swedroe, Larry, "The Costs of Active Management," Money-Watch, September 7, 2009. Available at www.moneywatch.bnet.com/investing/blog/wise-investing/the-costs-of-active-management/826.

An excellent article describing closet index funds is Lewis Braham, "How to Spot a Closet Index Fund," *Bloomberg Businessweek*, September 6, 2004. Available at www.businessweek.com/magazine/content/04_36/b3898134_mz070.htm.

The *Wall Street Journal* identified some closet index funds in this article: Sam Mamudi, "What Are You Paying For?," *Wall Street Journal*, December 8, 2009. Available at http://online.wsj.com/article/SB10001424052748704402404574529550789419572.html.

The staggering amount of investments in closet index funds is set forth in this study: Martijn Cremers and Antti Petajisto, "How Active

Is Your Fund Manager? A New Measure That Predicts Performance," AFA 2007 Chicago Meetings Paper, EFA 2007 Ljubljana Meetings Paper, Yale ICF Working Paper No. 06-14, March 31, 2009. Available at www.ssrn.com/abstract=891719.

14. Superior Returns Are Within Your Grasp

The study that set forth the returns of the average stock investor is the Dalbar QAIB study. It is available only for purchase at www.dalbar .com. However, it is extensively cited and discussed: Dalbar summarized the findings of its 2010 study in a press release issued March 31, 2010, as follows: "For the 20-year period, equity fund investors averaged 3.17% compared to 8.20% for buy-and-hold stock investors (S&P 500)." Available at www.dalbarinc.com/Portals/dalbar/cache/ News/PressReleases/pressrelease20100331.pdf. See also "Dalbar Update: Investors Still Lagging the Market," InvestorsInsight.com. Available at http://investorsinsight.com/blogs/forecasts_trends/archive/2009/11/ 03/dalbar-update-investors-still-lagging-the-market.aspx.

Helpful charts summarizing the Dalbar study can be found at www.ifa.com/12steps/step1/Dalbar.asp.

15. The Right Focus

The Brinson, Hood, and Beebower study is available at www.ifa .com/pdf/Determinants_of_Portfolio_Performance.pdf.

You can find an asset allocation questionnaire at www.smartestin vestmentbook.com. Click on "Asset Allocation Questionnaire." You can take either the short (5-question) or the complete (25-question) Risk Capacity Survey. The results of either one will assist you in determining the right division between stocks and bonds for your portfolio.

Treasury bills are issued by the U.S. Department of the Treasury. They are backed by the full faith and credit of the U.S. government and mature in one year or less.

You can confirm if a bank is FDIC insured by using the "Bank Find" tool on the FDIC's website: www2.fdic.gov/idasp/main_bankfind.asp. The interview with Tavis Smiley, on November 13, 2009, is available from PBS at www.pbs.org/wnet/tavissmiley/archive/200911/20091113_zweig.html.

A respected colleague prefers a supplemental term when discussing the possibility of black swans. He refers to "green swans" to convey the fact that the possibility of an extraordinarily *positive* event is every bit as likely as a negative one.

16. Taxes and Costs: Stealth Enemies

John Bogle's analysis of the after-tax returns of active and passive investors is set forth in his excellent book *The Little Book of Common Sense Investing* (Wiley: Hoboken, NJ, 2007).

The Dickson and Shoven study is Joel M. Dickson and John B. Shoven, "Taxation and Mutual Funds: An Investor Perspective." Available at www.nber.org/chapters/c10894.pdf.

For a good introduction to ETFs, see Ken Hawkins, "Exchange-Trade Funds: Introduction," Investopedia. Available at www.investopedia.com/university/exchange-traded-fund. See also Dan Culloton, "Are ETFs Really More Tax-Efficient Than Mutual Funds?," *Morningstar Advisor*, February 14, 2006. Available at www.advisor.morningstar.com/articles/fcarticle.asp?s=&docId=4338&pgNo=0.

The benefits of Vanguard's ETFs are set forth in a brochure titled "Making the Case for Vanguard ETFs." Available at www.advisors.vanguard.com/iwe/pdf/FASETFB.pdf.

For an in-depth discussion of the tax efficiency of ETFs in general, and specifically Vanguard ETFs, see Sigma Investing's "ETF Tax Efficiency." The article discusses both sides of the issue of whether Vanguard's ETFs are more efficient than are its competitors' due to their different structure. Available at www.sigmainvesting.com/tax-management/etf-tax-efficiency.

A chart showing the estimated capital gains for all Vanguard ETFs as of November 30, 2009, is available at www.advisors.vanguard.com/VGApp/iip/site/advisor/researchcommentary/news/article?File=IWE_NewsAllCapGainsUpdate122009.

17. Rebalancing: Sense and Nonsense

There are a dizzying number of recommendations for rebalancing. Here's a sampling:

Arnott, Robert D., and Robert M. Lovell Jr., "Rebalancing: Why? When? How Often?," *Journal of Investing*, spring 1993. Available at http://classic-web.archive.org/web/20050213200611/http://www.firstquadrant.com/PDFs/Monographs/9203mono.pdf.

"The Art of Rebalancing: How to Tell When Your Portfolio Needs a Tune-up," Smith Barney Group, 2005. Available at www.asaecenter.org/files/ArtofRebalancing.pdf.

Daryanani, Gobind, "Opportunistic Rebalancing: A New Paradigm for Wealth Managers," *Journal of Financial Planning*, January 2008. Available at www.tdainstitutional.com/pdf/Opportunistic_Rebalancing_JFP2007_Daryanani.pdf.

Leland, Hayne E., "Optimal Asset Rebalancing in the Presence of Transactions," working paper series, RPF-261, August 1996. Available at www.ssrn.com/abstract=1060.

Masters, Seth J., "Rules for Rebalancing," December 1, 2002. Available at http://web.archive.org/web/20071027064945/http://www.financial-planning.com/pubs/fp/20021201018.html.

The views of Vanguard on rebalancing can be found in this paper: Yesim Tokat, "Portfolio Rebalancing in Theory and Practice," Vanguard

Investment Counseling & Research, 2006. Available at https://institu
tional.vanguard.com/iip/pdf/ICRRebalancing.pdf.

19. Fama and French Are SuperSmart

You can access Eugene Fama's website at http://faculty.chicago
booth.edu/eugene.fama.

Fama's thesis, titled "Random Walks in Stock Market Price," is
available at www.ifa.com/Media/Images/PDF%20files/FamaRandom
Walk.pdf.

For a succinct definition of the efficient market hypothesis, see
"Efficient Market Hypothesis," Investopedia. Available at www.investo
pedia.com/terms/e/efficientmarkethypothesis.asp.

The earliest version of the random walk theory is generally attrib-
uted to Louis Bachelier, who set forth the following observation in his
doctoral thesis in 1900: "The influences that determine the movements
of the exchange are innumerable; past, current and even anticipated
events that often have no obvious connection with its changes . . . it is
thus impossible to hope for mathematical predictability." Louis Bachelier, "Théorie de la Spéculation," *Annales Scientifique de l'École Normale
Supérieure*, 3rd series, 17 (1900): 21–86.

Ken French's curriculum vitae lists his publications. Available at
http://mba.tuck.dartmouth.edu/pages/faculty/ken.french/curricu
lum_vitae.html.

For speculation about Fama and French winning the Nobel Prize,
see the following:

Fletcher, Emily, "Prof. Named as Likely Nobel Prize Contender,"
Dartmouth, October 9, 2009. Available at http://thedartmouth.com/
2009/10/09/news/nobel.

Hall of Citation Laureates, Economics, Thomson Reuters. Available
at www.science.thomsonreuters.com/nobel/categories/economics.

Morgan, Sarah, "Who Will Win the Nobel Prize in Economics?," SmartMoney, October 9, 2009. Available at www.smartmoney.com/investing/economy/who-will-win-the-nobel-prize-in-economics.

For a detailed explanation of the Fama-French three-factor model, see www.ifa.com/12steps/step8/step8page4.asp. See also "Fama and French Three Factor Model," Moneychimp.com (www.moneychimp.com/articles/risk/multifactor.htm) and Kent L. Womack and Ying Zhang, "Understanding Risk and Return, the CAPM, and the Fama-French Three-Factor Model," Tuck Case No. 03-111, December 19, 2003 (www.ssrn.com/abstract=481881).

There is a wealth of data supporting the acceptance of the Fama-French three-factor model. Here is a representative sampling of the studies endorsing this model:

Armstrong, Frank, "Fama-French Three Factor Model, Part 1," Investor Solutions Incorporated, 2003. Available at www.dethomasfinancial.com/newsletters/FamaFrench_ThreeFactorReview1.pdf.

- "The Three Factor Model has replaced Capital Asset Pricing Model (CAPM) as the most widely accepted explanation of stock prices in the aggregate and investor returns."

Bickford, Joel D., "Fama/French Three Factor Model," Bickford Investment Management Services. Available at www.bickfordinvest.com/fctr0401.pdf.

- "At this point in time, the Fama/French Three Factor Model is generally accepted and is taught in all of the top U.S. business schools."

Chou, Pin-Huang, Robin K. Chou, and Jane-Sue Wang, "On the Cross-Section of Expected Stock Returns: Fama-French Ten Years Later," *Finance Letter* 2 (1) (2004): 18–22. Available at www.mgt.ncu.edu.tw/~chou/ff10years.pdf.

- "The seminal work of Fama and French (1992), however, identified market value (size) and the ratio of book to market equity (BM) as the two major determinants of the cross-sectional expected returns, and sentenced the 'death' of beta."

"Multi-Period Asset Allocation," Modern Investment Technologies. Available at http://smartfolio.fileburst.com/download/Theory%20Help.pdf.

- "The asset pricing model, developed by Eugene Fama and Kenneth French, is widely accepted as one of the most successful Factor-based Asset-Pricing Models ever created."

Ruzita Abdul Rahim and Abu Hassan Shaari Mohd Nor, "A Comparison Between Fama-French Model and Liquidity-Based Three Factor Models in Predicting the Portfolio Returns," *Asian Academy of Management Journal of Accounting and Finance* 2 (2) (2006).

- "Since its introduction in 1993, Fama-French model has been extensively attended to the extent that it is currently considered the workhorse for risk adjustment in academic circles."

"Three Factor Model for Portfolio Management," Buzzle.com. Available at www.buzzle.com/articles/three-factor-model-for-portfolio-management.html.

- "Three Factor Model, popularly known as Fama and French three-factor model, is one of the most followed portfolio management models. . . . Three-factor model is widely followed by investors and fund managers to analyze risk and return associated with instruments/markets and to make highest return for risk taken."

Womack, Kent L., and Zhang, Ying, "Understanding Risk and Return, the CAPM, and the Fama-French Three-Factor Model," Tuck Case No. 03-111, December 19, 2003. Available at http://papers.ssrn.com/sol3/papers.cfm?abstract_id=481881.

- "The three factors in concert explain most of the returns due to risk exposure."

The following is a representative list of papers criticizing the Fama-French three-factor model:

Black, Fischer, "Beta and Return," *Journal of Portfolio Management* 20 (1) (fall 1993). Available at www.docstoc.com/docs/7752493/Beta-and-Return.

Foster, F. Douglas, Tom M. Smith, and Robert E. Whaley, "Assessing Goodness-of-Fit of Asset Pricing Models: The Distribution of the Maximal R2," *Journal of Finance* 52 (2) (June 1997). Available at http://ssrn.com/abstract=3782.

Knez, Peter J., and Mark J. Ready, "On the Robustness of Size and Book-to-Market in Cross-Sectional Regressions," *Journal of Finance* 52 (4) (September 1997). Available at www.jstor.org/pss/2329439.

Lakonishok, Josef, Andrei Shleifer, and Robert W. Vishny, "Contrarian Investment, Extrapolation, and Risk," NBER Working Paper No. W4360 (May 1993). Available at http://ssrn.com/abstract=227016.

Loughran, Tim, "Book-to-Market Across Firm Size, Exchange, and Seasonality: Is There an Effect?," *Journal of Financial and Quantitative Analysis* 32 (3) (September 1997). Available at www.jstor.org/pss/2331199.

Mackinlay, Craig, "Multifactor Models Do Not Explain Deviations from the CAPM," *Journal of Financial Economics* 69 (5) (1995): 1541–1578. Available at www.nber.org/papers/w4360.pdf.

Fama responds to critics in Eugene Fama Jr., "Professor Fama Answers the Critics," Index Funds Advisors, December 1, 1999. Available at www.ifa.com/articles/Professor_Fama_Answers_the_Critics.aspx.

A strong proponent of EMH, Burton Malkiel (author of the investment classic *A Random Walk Down Wall Street*) dealt with critics of the Fama-French three-factor model in this paper: Burton G. Malkiel, "The Efficient Market Hypothesis and Its Critics," CEPS Working Paper No. 91, April 2003. Available at www.princeton.edu/~ceps/workingpapers/91malkiel.pdf.

Videos of interviews with Eugene Fama and Kenneth French can be viewed at www.indexfunds.com/flash/FrenchKenhifi.flv, www.ifa.com/advisorcam, and www.ifa.com/Media/Video/FullVideos/Eugene Fama/dimensional_thinkers_fama_250k.flv.

For a discussion of the relative risk of value and growth stocks, see Lu Zhang, "The Value Premium," Simon School of Business Working Paper No. FR 02-19 (November 13, 2002). Available at http://ssrn.com/abstract=351060. Zhang notes that "assets-in-place or value is riskier than growth option in bad times and growth option is as risky as or slightly riskier than assets-in-place in good times."

20. The SuperSmart Portfolio: Designed to Produce Higher Returns

Constructing this portfolio required sophisticated expertise in financial engineering. The financial engineering was done by Edward S. O'Neal, PhD, with assistance from Sean Kelly. The methodology used to construct the SuperSmart Portfolio is set forth in Appendix A.

The appropriate allocation between domestic and international stocks is discussed in Christopher B. Philips, "International Equity: Considerations and Recommendations," Vanguard Investment Counseling & Research, 2006. Available at www.institutional.vanguard.com/iip/pdf/ICRIECR.pdf. The author of this study concluded: "Although no absolute answer exists for all investors, it should be clear that an allocation range of 20% to 40% is reasonable given the historical benefits of diversification."

You can learn more about the Sharpe ratio in a three-part blog post series: Dr. Kris, "Spotlight on the Sharpe Ratio," *Seeking Alpha*, November 5, 2009. Available at http://seekingalpha.com/article/171438-spotlight-on-the-sharpe-ratio-part-i.

Here is an example of how the Sharpe ratio can be helpful to investors. This example is based on one given in "Understanding the Sharpe Ratio," Investopedia. Available at www.investopedia.com/articles/07/sharpe_ratio.asp.

Let's assume you are considering two mutual funds. One is managed by Bill Picker. It has a return of 12%. The other is managed by Sally Passive. Hers had a return of only 8%. Should you assume Picker is a better fund manager than is Passive?

What if Picker is taking more risk than Passive? Don't you want to know how much the two funds returned in relation to the amount of risk they took?

The amount of risk should be a critical factor in your decision because an investment with a higher return but with significantly higher risk will have a higher risk of loss. You need to determine if the possibility of additional return is worth the additional risk. You want to avoid the possibility of a *low* return with a *high* risk.

The Sharpe ratio will give you the answer. To compute it, you need to know two facts: (1) What's the risk-free rate of return of a short-term Treasury bill? Remember, the Sharpe ratio measures the *excess* return you are getting over the risk-free rate of return. If you are going to take more risk, you want to be sure you are compensated for it. Let's assume the risk-free rate of return is 2%. (2) What is the risk of the two funds? This is critical because you need to understand how much risk you are taking. If a gold fund has five times the risk of a value fund, but both have the same historical returns, your investing decision is simple. You won't "go for the gold."

Standard deviation is expressed as a percentage. The higher the percentage, the riskier the asset. Let's assume the standard deviation of the Picker fund is 20% and the standard deviation of the Passive fund is 8%. Clearly, the Passive fund has less risk.

Now let's compute the Sharpe ratio of the funds managed by Picker and Passive.

The Sharpe ratio can be computed by taking the average return, deducting the risk-free rate of return, and dividing by the standard deviation.

For Picker, take his 12% return, deduct the 2% risk-free rate of return, and divide by the risk of his fund as measured by the standard deviation, which is 20%. The Sharpe ratio for his fund is 0.50.

For Passive, take her 8% return, deduct the 2% risk-free rate of return, and divide by the risk of her fund as measured by the standard deviation, which is 8%. The Sharpe ratio for her fund is 0.75.

Passive generated more returns on a risk-adjusted basis, meaning that, for the amount of risk investors assumed in Passive's fund, they got better returns than did investors in Picker's fund. Picker's investors got better absolute returns, but they took excess risk to get them.

It may, or may not, be in your best interest to take on additional risk to have the possibility of achieving the 4% higher returns Picker has produced. It would make a lot of sense to compute the Sharpe ratio for other comparable funds, with returns similar to Picker's, and select the one with the highest Sharpe ratio. More risk means more volatility and the greater possibility of loss.

Optimization programs, such as the one customized for use in constructing the SuperSmart Portfolio, are notoriously apt to produce strange and nonintuitive allocations unless they are constrained by specified maximum and minimum allocations to each asset class. This factor was taken into account in the construction of the SuperSmart Portfolio.

23. The Smartest Target Date Portfolio

For a discussion of the growth of target date funds, see Josh Charlson, David Falkof, Michael Herbst, Laura Pavlenko Lutton, and John Rekenthaler, "Target-Date Series Research Paper: 2010 Industry Survey," Morningstar, 2010. Available at www.corporate.morningstar

.com/US/documents/MethodologyDocuments/MethodologyPapers/ TargetDateFundSurvey_2010.pdf.

For some additional tips about picking the right target date fund, see Tara Siegel Bernard, "Target Date Funds: Seven Questions to Ask Before Jumping In," *New York Times*, June 28, 2009. Available at www.nytimes .com/2009/06/29/your-money/mutual-funds-and-etfs/29target.html.

Detailed information about Vanguard's target date funds can be found on its website (vanguard.com) and in its brochure: Scott J. Donaldson, C. William Cole, Francis M. Kinniry Jr., John Ameriks, Roger Aliaga-Díaz, and Anatoly Shtekhman, "Vanguard's Approach to Target-Date Funds." Available at https://personal.vanguard.com/us/Literature Request?FW_Activity=ViewOnlineActivity&litID=2210051169&FW_Event =start&view_mode=web&usage_cat2=&viewLitID=2210051169 &formName=Investments-+Vanguards+approach+to+target-date +funds&vendorID=S167&cbdForceDomain=false.

Returns before and after taxes for the Vanguard Target Retirement 2015 Fund can be found on Vanguard's website: https://personal.van guard.com/us/funds/snapshot?FundId=0303&FundIntExt=INT#hist= tab%3A1.

Information about Fidelity's Freedom Index Funds is available on its website at http://personal.fidelity.com/products/funds/content/ DesignYourPortfolio/target_timelinefunds_freedom.shtml.cvsr? refpr=mfrt16.

Information about TIAA-CREF's Lifecycle Index Funds is available in its 2010 Annual Report. Available at http://tiaa-cref.org/ucm/groups/ content/@ap_ucm_p_tcp_inco/documents/document/tiaa01011326 .pdf.

The Fidelity Freedom 2020 Fund (FFDC) has an expense ratio of 0.74%; see http://fundresearch.fidelity.com/mutual-funds/summary/ 31617R605.

The expense ratio of TIAA-CREF's Lifecycle Funds can be found in "2010 Annual Report: TIAA CREF Lifecycle Funds," September 30,

2010, p. 6. Available at http://tiaa-cref.org/ucm/groups/content/ @ap_ucm_p_tcp_inco/documents/document/tiaa01007810.pdf.

John Bogle's quip about investors paying for the excessive costs of active management can be found in John C. Bogle's "In Investing, You Get What You *Don't* Pay For," World Money Show, February 2, 2005. Available at www.vanguard.com/bogle_site/sp20050202.htm.

24. The Smartest ETF Portfolio

For an explanation of the FTSE All-World Index, see its website at www.ftse.com/Indices/FTSE_All_World_Index_Series/index.jsp.

Information about the Vanguard Total World Stock Index ETF can be found on Vanguard's website at http://personal.vanguard.com/us/ funds/snapshot?FundId=3141&FundIntExt=INT#hist=tab%3A0.

For information about the iShares MSCI ACWI (All Country World) Index, see its website at www.mscibarra.com/products/indices/ global_equity_indices/definitions.html.

For a view that an allocation as high as 50% to international stocks is optimal, see Larry Swedroe, "Low Cost Diversification with Vanguard Total World Stock Index ETF (VT)?," *Moolanomy*, February 9, 2009. Available at www.moolanomy.com/1242/low-cost-diversification-with -vanguard-total-world-stock-etf-vt.

Details of the allocation of the iShares MSCI ACWI Index Fund can be found in a fact sheet for the fund that is available at its website at http://us.ishares.com/content/stream.jsp?url=/content/en_us/ repository/resource/fact_sheet/acwi.pdf&mimeType=application/ pdf.

For a discussion of the merits of a globally diversified bond portfolio, see Yvette Klevan and Jared Daniels, "Fixed Income: The Benefits of Global Diversification and Active Investing," Lazard, 2008, p. 2. Available at www.lazardnet.com/lam/us/tpd/pdfs/FixedIncome_Benefits.pdf.

The total value of the world bond market in 2009 was $82 trillion. The U.S. share of that market was $31 trillion or 37.9%. Albert

J. Brenner, "World Stock and Bond Markets and Portfolio Diversity," Asset Allocation Advisor. November 15, 2009. Available at www .aametrics.com/pdfs/world_stock_and_bond_markets_nov2009.pdf.

There is a helpful chart comparing U.S. and foreign government bond returns in this article: "The Bond Market: A Look Back," Investopedia. Available at www.investopedia.com/articles/06/centuryofbonds.asp.

In a document by Yvette Klevan and Jared Daniels, "Fixed Income: The Benefits of Global Diversification and Active Investing," Lazard Asset Management, 2008, the authors conclude: "We believe that active global fixed-income investing offers the potential for a more attractive risk/return profile than domestic fixed income, because of the expanded opportunity set, the possibility to invest in low-correlated markets, and the ability to add value through currency management." Available at www.lazardnet.com/lam/us/tpd/pdfs/FixedIncome_Benefits.pdf.

Another study found that "global bond funds provide higher total returns and comparable risk-adjusted returns to U.S.-based bond funds that invest only in U.S. bond markets (i.e., domestic bond funds)" and "for U.S. investors whose portfolios are concentrated in domestic bond funds, adding global bond funds to the portfolios can enhance the return by 0.5% to 1% per year without increasing risk." Sirapat Polwitoon and Oranee Tawatnuntachai, "Diversification Benefits and Persistence of U.S.-Based Global Bond Funds," May 2005. Available at www.efmaefm.org/efma2005/papers/202-polwitoon_paper.pdf.

27. Asking the Wrong Question

Many investors understand the data supporting index investing of the stock portion of their portfolio but persist in an active strategy for bonds. An article in the *Wall Street Journal* noted that, in 2008, the average intermediate bond fund lost 4.7% while the Barclays Capital Aggregate Index (tracked by many bond index funds) gained 5.2%. The article also noted that, since 1999, there has been only one year when the average bond fund topped the index. Tom Lauricella, "No Diversification: How Bond Funds Let Investors Down," *Wall Street Journal*, July 8, 2009. Available at http://online.wsj.com/article/SB10001 4240529702033343043574163793909392038.html.

For a discussion of the relationship between low fees and higher returns, see "Today's Research Question: Why Do Investors Choose High-Fee Mutual Funds Despite the Lower Returns?," Knowledge at Wharton, May 31, 2006. Available at http://knowledge.wharton.upenn .edu/article.cfm?articleid=1491. "Clearly, investors have embraced the core belief that minimizing annual fees boosts long-term gains." And the authors noted the anomaly that "investors persist in holding trillions of dollars in high-fee funds despite the well-publicized evidence that low-fee alternatives offer higher returns over the long run."

I obtained data about the number of households owning stocks or bonds from "Equity and Bond Ownership in America, 2008," Investment Company Institute and the Securities Industry and Financial Markets Association, 2008, p. 2. Available at www.ici.org/pdf/rpt_08 _equity_owners.pdf.

The text of the Uniform Prudent Investor Act can be found at www .law.upenn.edu/bll/archives/ulc/fnact99/1990s/upia94.pdf.

A map of the states that have adopted the Uniform Prudent Investor Act can be found at www.nccusl.org/Act.aspx?title=Prudent Investor Act.

For an informative discussion of the differences between ERISA fiduciaries, see W. Scott Simon, "The Different Flavors of ERISA Fiduciaries," *Morningstar Advisor*, December 3, 2009. Available at www .advisor.morningstar.com/articles/fcarticle.asp?docId=17902.

29. An Unlikely Source of Returns

Data and sources setting forth returns captured by investors with and without advisers is summarized at the Index Funds Advisors' website: www.ifa.com/Section/Passive_Investing_and_Good_Advice.asp.

30. Don't Confuse Knowledge with Success

Data on bond flows can be found at "Bond-Fund Flows at an All-Time Peak," Morgan Stanley, slide no. 5, data as of December 10, 2009. Available at www.authorstream.com/Presentation/slidea-373897-Morgan -Stanley-Entertainment-ppt-powerpoint.

For a good primer on tax loss harvesting, with examples of how it works, see James Lange, "Tax Loss Harvesting," PayTaxesLater.com. Available at www.paytaxeslater.com/tax_loss_harvesting.htm.

31. The Dimensional Difference

The Dimensional Fund Advisors' website is www.dfaus.com.

A list of academics affiliated with DFA is available at www.dfaus .com/firm/academics.html.

Find a partial list of DFA's clients at www.dfaus.com/firm/clients .html.

For a discussion of the differences between a portfolio of DFA funds and ETFs, see "Dimensionals vs. ETFs," Dimensional, July 2004. Available at www.abacuswealth.com/resources/dfavsetfs.pdf.

The study comparing returns of DFA with those of Vanguard is Edward Tower and Cheng-Ying Yang, "Enhanced Versus Passive Mutual Fund Indexing: Has DFA Outperformed Vanguard by Enough to Justify Its Advisor and Transaction Fees?," *The Journal of Investing*, winter 2008. A working draft of this paper is available at www.econ.duke .edu/Papers/PDF/Vanguard_Versus_DFA_30 july_2007.pdf.

Professor Tower kindly provided me with a copy of his subsequent study. It appears as part of a chapter in *Mutual Funds: Portfolio Structures, Analysis, Management, and Stewardship*, ed. John A. Haslem (Wiley: Hoboken, NJ, 2009).

Glossary

active fund managers: Managers who rely on research and their own judgment in making investment decisions. Their goal is to exceed the returns of a designated benchmark, like the S&P 500 index.

ADV report: An SEC requirement for registration of investment advisers. It contains personal and business information about the registrant.

alpha: The value added by a portfolio manager, above what you would expect, given the level of risk taken. Alpha can be positive or negative. If it is negative, the manager has subtracted value due to his management activities.

annuities: Contracts sold by insurance companies that provide for payments at fixed intervals. Annuities can be fixed or variable. All annuities are tax deferred.

arithmetic annual returns: The sum of a series of returns, divided by the number of that series of numbers.

asset allocation: The process of dividing your investments between stocks, bonds, and cash.

auction rate securities: Bonds sold though Dutch auctions (which start with a high interest rate and go down until the rate is fixed). The interest rate was supposed to be reset periodically.

black swan event: An extraordinary, negative occurrence that is random and unpredictable.

bonds: Debt instruments issued by companies or governments for the purpose of raising capital by borrowing. The issuer of the bond promises to repay the principal with interest on a specified date.

book-to-market ratio: Compares the book value of a company to its market value.

book value: The net asset value of a company computed by deducting its liabilities and intangible assets from its assets.

buy and hold: Refers to the investing strategy of buying stocks and holding them for long time periods while ignoring short-term market fluctuations.

certificates of deposit: A financial product offered to consumers by banks, thrift institutions, and credit unions. Typically, they pay interest at a stated rate for a fixed term. If they are insured by the FDIC, they are backed by the full faith and credit of the U.S. government.

closet index funds: Refers to mutual funds in which the fund manager purchases most of the stocks in the index he or she is supposed to beat.

correlation: The extent to which the values of different types of investments move in tandem with one another in response to changing economic and market conditions.

currency hedging: A strategy that reduces currency risk by employing trading strategies that minimize the risk.

currency risk: Refers to the change in the value of one currency against another.

DFA: Refers to Dimensional Fund Advisors (dfaus.com), a mutual fund family that disavows the belief that markets are mistaken. It uses custom-designed indexes to capture the risk factors that explain 95% of market returns.

diversification: Refers to the inclusion of a wide variety of investments within a portfolio. It is used to yield higher returns, with a lower risk, than concentrating investments in a small number of securities.

Dow Jones Industrial Average (DJIA): An index consisting of 30 blue-chip stocks. It is the price-weighted average of these stocks. *Price weighted* means the index is weighted by the market price of each security. An uptick in a higher-priced stock will have more impact on the index average than an uptick in a lower-priced stock.

efficient market hypothesis: Holds that efforts to beat the market are futile because markets are efficient and stock prices instantly take into consideration all publicly available information about publicly traded securities.

enhanced indexing: A form of investing that uses the basic tools of passive investing but adds additional factors intended to improve returns over simply tracking a commercial index.

exchange-traded funds: Funds that track a designated index. They are traded like stocks and purchased and sold through brokers.

expected return: The estimated value of an investment. It's calculated using a probability distribution curve that considers all possible rates of return.

expense ratio: The measure of operating costs of a mutual fund, which includes management fees. It's usually expressed as a percent of the fund's average net assets.

Fama-French three-factor model: Sets forth three factors that explain the risk and return of diversified portfolios.

fundamental analysis: Involves research to determine the financial condition of a company. It typically includes a detailed study of financial information relating to the sales and operations of the company.

GDP: Refers to gross domestic product. It is used to measure the economic growth of a country.

geometric average annual returns: Takes into account the fact that the returns you earn in one year affect what you earn in subsequent years because returns are compounded over time.

global market capitalization: The total dollar market value of all the publicly traded securities in the global economy. It is computed by multiplying the number of outstanding shares by the price of one share of stock.

Great Depression: A worldwide economic collapse that occurred in 1929. It was followed by an extended period of high unemployment and business failures.

growth stocks: Refers to stocks that have significant earnings, evidencing rapid growth, beyond the growth of the overall economy. They typically pay no dividends because they reinvest in their own companies.

halo effect: Refers to the tendency to form an overall opinion about a person based on a perception in one area.

hedge funds: Funds that use strategies like selling short, swaps, and arbitrage in an effort to achieve high returns. They are used by wealthy and sophisticated individuals and institutions.

index funds: Mutual funds that track a designated market index, like the S&P 500 index.

junk bonds: High-risk bonds with a low credit rating. They typically offer high yields.

lack of correlation: Refers to securities or asset classes that are not likely to move in the same direction at the same time.

laddered bond portfolio: Consists of bonds with different maturities. It is used to provide a steady stream of income and to moderate interest rate fluctuations. Typically, the investor holds the bonds to maturity.

late trading: Trading shares in a mutual fund after the close of the trading day, which is illegal but occurred at several mutual fund families in the late 1990s and early 2000s.

Madoff, Bernie: The former chairman of NASDAQ who pleaded guilty to swindling more than $50 billion from investors in a fraudulent Ponzi scheme in 2009.

market capitalization: Calculated by multiplying the number of a company's outstanding shares by its share price.

market timing: Attempting to predict the future direction of the stock or bond markets.

money market funds: Funds that pay interest to shareholders and seek to maintain a net asset value of $1 per share. They typically invest in short-term, high-quality, liquid debt.

negative alpha: The value subtracted by a portfolio manager due to his management activities. Portfolios with a negative alpha underperform their benchmark indexes.

neuroeconomics: Refers to efforts to understand how the function of the brain affects decision making.

passive management: A style of investing where the portfolio mirrors a market index.

Ponzi scheme: A scam where a promoter uses money from new investors to pay illusory profits to old investors.

principal-protected notes: Fixed income securities that supposedly guarantee a minimum return equal to the initial investment while permitting investors to potentially profit from favorable market movements. The reality is quite different.

private equity funds: Typically limited partnerships, in which the private equity firm acts as the general partner. Accredited investors fund the investment(s) of the partnership.

rebalancing: The process of adjusting your portfolio to account for changes in the original asset allocation, due to market performance.

reinvestment: Refers to the use of dividends or interest to purchase more of an investment.

risk-adjusted return: A measure of how much of a return you are likely to receive on an investment in relation to the amount of risk you undertake.

S&P 500 index: An index that consists of 500 stocks weighted by market value. It is often incorrectly used as a benchmark for the performance of the U.S. stock market.

Sharpe ratio: A calculation that measures performance after taking risk into account.

small cap stocks: Stocks with a small market capitalization, typically between $300 million and $2 billion.

spot price: Refers to the current delivery price of gold as traded on the spot market. It is also referred to as the cash price.

spread: The difference between the current bid and the current ask price of a bond.

standard deviation: A statistical measure of the historical volatility of a stock, mutual fund, or portfolio. It measures how much the year-by-year returns of a stock (or a fund or a portfolio) deviate from its average annual return. Although standard deviation can be calculated over any period (daily, weekly, monthly), it's usually expressed as an annualized number. A volatile stock will have a high standard deviation and will be considered risky. A Treasury bill will be less volatile (with a low standard deviation) and will be considered less risky.

stock picking: The process of selecting a stock believed to be a superior investment compared to other stocks.

subprime mortgages: Mortgages given to borrowers with low credit scores.

target date funds: Mutual funds that automatically change their mix of assets between stocks and bonds to become more conservative each year.

tax loss harvesting: A process by which securities are sold at a loss and the loss is used to offset future capital gains tax liability.

ticker symbol: A symbol that uniquely identifies a publicly traded stock or mutual fund.

Treasury bills: Short-term debt obligations (less than one year) backed by the full faith and credit of the U.S. government.

uncompensated risk: Risk that can be eliminated through diversification. Investors are not rewarded with higher expected returns for taking this type of risk.

Uniform Prudent Investor Act: A statute that governs the conduct of investment fiduciaries.

value stocks: Stocks that are considered undervalued when the share price is compared to the underlying fundamentals, like book value, sales, and earnings.

variability of returns: Refers to a potential range of outcomes. For example, a company's stock may increase by 50% in one year, but decrease by the same amount (or more) in the following year. Its returns would be highly variable. The returns of a bond investment would typically not fluctuate as widely from year to year under normal conditions. The bond would exhibit a lower variability of returns.

APPENDIX A

Constructing the SuperSmart Portfolio

The first step in building the SuperSmart Portfolio is predicated on the fact that the most important factor in determining the variability of investment returns is a portfolio's exposure to the stock market or *market* factor.

The exposure to the stock market in a given portfolio can range between 0% and 100%. The SuperSmart Portfolio has five levels of risk, ranging from 20% exposure to stocks (lowest risk) to 100% (highest risk). Exposure to the stock market includes both domestic stocks and foreign stocks. Exposure to foreign stocks (including emerging markets) is important because of the data indicating that inclusion of this asset class can reduce the risk of a portfolio while maintaining the same expected return.

Within the stock portion of a portfolio, there are two types of stocks that historically have offered higher returns than the broad market, albeit with incrementally higher risk: small stocks and value stocks. The stock portion of the SuperSmart Portfolio is tilted to include more small stocks and more value stocks than would be typical for a broad-based, internationally diversified stock market portfolio. The goal is to tilt the portfolio toward these classes of stocks to the point at which the added risk is fully compensated with added return. The published research refers to tilting the portfolio toward these stocks as weighting the *size* factor and the *value* factor.

To select stock funds to provide the most advantageous exposure to the three important factors (market factor, size factor, and value factor), and to assign allocations to them, required the development of a portfolio optimization program to identify the combination of domestic, foreign, and emerging market stocks; value and growth stocks; and small and large stocks, which would maximize the historical return for any given level of risk.

The portion of the SuperSmart Portfolio not invested in the stock market is held in short- to medium-term U.S. and foreign government bonds. The SuperSmart Portfolio does not have exposure to longer-term bonds or to bonds with more credit risk than government bonds. Research demonstrates that increases in risk to a portfolio are most efficiently implemented by varying the exposure to stocks and not by varying the term or the credit risk of the bonds in a portfolio.

The data inputted into the optimization program was monthly return data for each class of stock and bonds from January 1970 to November 2010, with two exceptions. Due to lack of historical data, the real estate returns begin in January 1978 and the emerging market returns begin in January 1988.

The optimization program generated the allocations shown for each of the risk levels in the SuperSmart Portfolio.

APPENDIX B

Raw Data Used to Produce Risks and Returns

The following tables show the raw data used to produce the risk and return data for each of the Smartest Portfolios. The percentage listed after each index represents a fee deduction from the actual returns on an annual basis.

THE SUPERSMART PORTFOLIO: 20 YEARS

Vanguard Large Cap Index Admiral Fund	Actual fund returns 2005–2010 (Russell 1000 Index: 0.25% per year) 1991–2004
Vanguard Value Index Admiral Fund	Actual fund returns 1993–2010 (Russell 1000 Value Index: 0.25% per year) 1991–1992
Vanguard Small Cap Value ETF	Actual ETF returns 2005–2010 (Russell 2000 Value Index: 0.35% per year), 1991–2004
Vanguard REIT Index Admiral Fund	Actual fund returns 1997–2010 (Wilshire REIT Index: 0.35% per year) 1991–1996
iShares MSCI EAFE Value ETF	Actual ETF returns 2006–2010 (MSCI EAFE Value Index Gross Dividends: 0.35% per year) 1991–2005
iShares MSCI EAFE Small Cap ETF	Actual ETF returns 2008–2010 (EAFE Small Cap Index Gross Dividends: 0.50% per year) 1999–2007 (EAFE Small Cap Index Price Only: 0.50% per year) 1993–1998 (MSCI World except U.S. Net Dividends Reinvested US Dollars: 0.50% per year) 1991–1992
Vanguard Emerging Markets Stock Index Admiral Fund	Actual fund returns 1995–2010 (MSCI Emerging Markets Index: 0.50% per year) 1991–1994

iShares Barclays Short Treasury Bond ETF	Actual ETF returns 2008–2010 (Merrill Lynch 1-Year U.S. Treasury Index: 0.1% per year) 1991–2007
iShares Barclays Capital Short-Term International Treasury Bond ETF	Actual ETF returns 2010 (Citi World Government Bond Index 1- to 3-Year, Unhedged: 0.25% per year) 1991–2009

THE SUPERSMART PORTFOLIO: 10 YEARS

Vanguard Large Cap Index Admiral Fund	Actual fund returns 2005–2010 (Russell 1000 Index: 0.25% per year) 2001–2004
Vanguard Value Index Admiral Fund	Actual fund returns 2001–2010
Vanguard Small Cap Value ETF	Actual ETF returns 2005–2010 (Russell 2000 Value Index: 0.35% per year) 2001–2004
Vanguard REIT Index Admiral Fund	Actual fund returns 2001–2010
iShares MSCI EAFE Value ETF	Actual ETF returns 2006–2010 (MSCI EAFE Value Index Gross Divs: 0.35% per year) 2001–2005
iShares MSCI EAFE Small Cap ETF	Actual ETF returns 2008–2010 (EAFE Small Cap Index Gross Divs: 0.50% per year) 2001–2007
Vanguard Emerging Markets Stock Index Admiral Fund	Actual fund returns 2001–2010
iShares Barclays Short Treasury Bond ETF	Actual ETF returns 2008–2010 (Merrill Lynch 1-Year U.S. Treasury Index: 0.10% per year) 2001–2007
iShares Barclays Capital Short-Term International Treasury Bond ETF	Actual ETF returns 2010 (Citi World Government Bond Index 1- to 3-Year, Unhedged: 0.25% per year) 2001–2009

THE SUPERSMART PORTFOLIO: 5 YEARS

Vanguard Large Cap Index Admiral Fund	Actual fund returns 2006–2010
Vanguard Value Index Admiral Fund	Actual fund returns 2006–2010
Vanguard Small Cap Value ETF	Actual ETF returns 2006–2010
Vanguard REIT Index Admiral Fund	Actual fund returns 2006–2010
iShares MSCI EAFE Value ETF	Actual ETF returns 2006–2010
iShares MSCI EAFE Small Cap ETF	Actual ETF returns 2008–2010 (EAFE Small Cap Index Gross Divs: 0.50% per year) 2006–2007

Vanguard Emerging Markets Stock Index Admiral Fund	Actual fund returns 2006–2010
iShares Barclays Short Treasury Bond ETF	Actual ETF returns 2008–2010 (Merrill Lynch 1-Year U.S. Treasury Index: 0.10% per year) 2006–2007
iShares Barclays Capital Short-Term International Treasury Bond ETF	Actual ETF returns 2010 (Citi World Government Bond Index 1- to 3-Year, Unhedged: 0.25% per year) 2006–2009

THE SUPERSMART PORTFOLIO: 3 YEARS

Vanguard Large Cap Index Admiral Fund	Actual fund returns 2008–2010
Vanguard Value Index Admiral Fund	Actual fund returns 2008–2010
Vanguard Small Cap Value ETF	Actual ETF returns 2008–2010
Vanguard REIT Index Admiral Fund	Actual fund returns 2008–2010
iShares MSCI EAFE Value ETF	Actual ETF returns 2008–2010
iShares MSCI EAFE Small Cap ETF	Actual ETF returns 2008–2010
Vanguard Emerging Markets Stock Index Admiral Fund	Actual fund returns 2008–2010
iShares Barclays Short Treasury Bond ETF	Actual ETF returns 2008–2010
iShares Barclays Capital Short-Term Inernational Treasury Bond ETF	Actual ETF returns 2010 (Citi World Government Bond Index 1- to 3-Year, Unhedged: 0.25% per year) 2008–2009

THE SMARTEST ETF PORTFOLIO: 20 YEARS

Vanguard Total World Stock Index ETF	Actual ETF returns 2009–2010 (FTSE All-World Total Return Index US Dollars: 0.30% per year) 1994–2008 (70% Russell 3000 Index, 30% MSCI EAFE Index: 0.30% per year) 1991–1993
iShares Barclays Short Treasury Bond ETF	Actual ETF returns 2008–2010 (Merrill Lynch 1-Year U.S. Treasury Index: 0.10% per year) 1991–2007
iShares Barclays Capital Short-Term International Treasury Bond ETF	Actual ETF returns 2010 (Citi World Government Bond Index 1- to 3-Year, Unhedged: 0.25% per year) 1991–2009

THE SMARTEST ETF PORTFOLIO: 10 YEARS

Vanguard Total World Stock Index ETF	Actual ETF returns 2009–2010 (FTSE All-World Total Return Index US Dollar: 0.30% per year) 2001–2008
iShares Barclays Short Treasury Bond ETF	Actual ETF returns 2008–2010 (Merrill Lynch 1-Year U.S. Treasury Index: 0.10% per year) 2001–2007
iShares Barclays Capital Short-Term International Treasury Bond ETF	Actual ETF returns 2010 (Citi World Government Bond Index 1- to 3-Year, Unhedged: 0.25% per year) 2001–2009

THE SMARTEST ETF PORTFOLIO: 5 YEARS

Vanguard Total World Stock Index ETF	Actual ETF returns 2009–2010 (FTSE All-World Total Return Index US Dollar: 0.30% per year) 2006–2008
iShares Barclays Short Treasury Bond ETF	Actual ETF returns 2008–2010 (Merrill Lynch 1-Year U.S. Treasury Index: 0.10% per year) 2006–2007
iShares Barclays Capital Short-Term International Treasury Bond ETF	Actual ETF returns 2010 (Citi World Government Bond Index 1- to 3-Year, Unhedged: 0.25% per year) 2006–2009

THE SMARTEST ETF PORTFOLIO: 3 YEARS

Vanguard Total World Stock Index ETF	Actual ETF returns 2009–2010 (FTSE All-World Total Return Index US Dollar: 0.30% per year) 2008
iShares Barclays Short Treasury Bond ETF	Actual ETF returns 2008–2010
iShares Barclays Capital Short-Term International Treasury Bond ETF	Actual ETF returns 2010 (Citi World Government Bond Index 1- to 3-Year, Unhedged: 0.25% per year) 2008–2009

THE SMARTEST INDEX FUND PORTFOLIO: 20 YEARS

Vanguard Total International Stock Index	Actual ETF returns 1997–2010 (MSCI EAFE Index: 0.35% per year) 1991–1996
Vanguard Total Stock Market Index	Actual fund returns 1993–2010 (Wilshire 5000 Index: 0.25% per year) 1991–1992
Vanguard Total Bond Market Index	Actual fund returns 1991–2010

THE SMARTEST INDEX FUND PORTFOLIO: 10 YEARS

Vanguard Total International Stock Index	Actual fund returns 2001–2010
Vanguard Total Stock Market Index	Actual fund returns 2001–2010
Vanguard Total Bond Market Index	Actual fund returns 2001–2010

THE SMARTEST INDEX FUND PORTFOLIO: 5 YEARS

Vanguard Total International Stock Index	Actual fund returns 2006–2010
Vanguard Total Stock Market Index	Actual fund returns 2006–2010
Vanguard Total Bond Market Index	Actual fund returns 2006–2010

THE SMARTEST INDEX FUND PORTFOLIO: 3 YEARS

Vanguard Total International Stock Index	Actual fund returns 2008–2010
Vanguard Total Stock Market Index	Actual fund returns 2008–2010
Vanguard Total Bond Market Index	Actual fund returns 2008–2010

APPENDIX C

Fidelity and T. Rowe Price Fund Options for the Smartest Index Fund Portfolio

Fidelity Funds

Fidelity funds that you could use to implement the Smartest Index Fund Portfolio are Fidelity Spartan Total Market Index Fund (FSTMX), the Fidelity Spartan International Index Fund (FSIIX), and the Fidelity U.S. Bond Index Fund (FBIDX). The following chart provides the disposition of the funds at five risk levels:

Fund	Low Risk	Medium-Low Risk	Medium Risk	Medium-High Risk	High Risk
FSTMX	14%	28%	42%	56%	70%
FSIIX	6%	12%	18%	24%	30%
FBIDX	80%	60%	40%	20%	0%

Risk and Return

FIDELITY FUNDS: RISK AND RETURN 20 YEARS

ALL PERFORMANCE DATA ARE EXPRESSED IN PERCENT AND ARE
HYPOTHETICAL INVESTMENT RESULTS FOR THE PERIOD 1991–2010.

Measure	Low Risk	Medium-Low Risk	Medium Risk	Medium-High Risk	High Risk
Average annual return (geometric)	7.44	7.94	8.30	8.50	8.51
Annualized standard deviation	5.86	8.46	11.71	15.20	18.81
Worst single-calendar-year period	−4.68	−13.13	−21.57	−30.01	−38.46
Worst two-calendar-year period	0.79	−7.84	−16.53	−25.27	−34.08
Worst three-calendar-year period	8.08	−0.50	−14.82	−27.71	−39.24

FIDELITY FUNDS: RISK AND RETURN 10 YEARS

ALL PERFORMANCE DATA ARE EXPRESSED IN PERCENT AND ARE
HYPOTHETICAL INVESTMENT RESULTS FOR THE PERIOD 2001–2010.

Measure	Low Risk	Medium-Low Risk	Medium Risk	Medium-High Risk	High Risk
Average annual return (geometric)	5.46	5.15	4.62	3.85	2.82
Annualized standard deviation	4.43	8.80	13.36	17.97	22.59
Worst single-calendar-year period	−4.68	−13.13	−21.57	−30.01	−38.46
Worst two-calendar-year period	0.79	−7.84	−16.53	−25.27	−34.08
Worst three-calendar-year period	8.08	1.51	−5.64	−13.35	−21.65

FIDELITY FUNDS: RISK AND RETURN 5 YEARS

ALL PERFORMANCE DATA ARE EXPRESSED IN PERCENT AND ARE
HYPOTHETICAL INVESTMENT RESULTS FOR THE PERIOD 2006–2010.

Measure	Low Risk	Medium-Low Risk	Medium Risk	Medium-High Risk	High Risk
Average annual return (geometric)	5.27	5.09	4.66	3.93	2.87
Annualized standard deviation	5.94	10.96	15.99	21.03	26.06
Worst single-calendar-year period	−4.68	−13.13	−21.57	−30.01	−38.46
Worst two-calendar-year period	0.79	−7.84	−16.53	−25.27	−34.08
Worst three-calendar-year period	8.08	1.51	−5.64	−13.35	−21.65

FIDELITY FUNDS: RISK AND RETURN 3 YEARS

ALL PERFORMANCE DATA ARE EXPRESSED IN PERCENT AND ARE
HYPOTHETICAL INVESTMENT RESULTS FOR THE PERIOD 2008–2010.

Measure	Low Risk	Medium-Low Risk	Medium Risk	Medium-High Risk	High Risk
Average annual return (geometric)	4.47	3.13	1.43	−0.68	−3.28
Annualized standard deviation	8.25	15.01	21.77	28.53	35.28
Worst single-calendar-year period	−4.68	−13.13	−21.57	−30.01	−38.46
Worst two-calendar-year period	5.65	0.11	−6.17	−13.20	−20.97
Worst three-calendar-year period	14.03	9.69	4.35	−2.04	−9.51

Raw Data

Here are the raw data used to produce the risk and return data for the Fidelity Fund Portfolios: Fidelity Spartan Total Market Index Fund (FSTMX), the Fidelity Spartan International Index Fund (FSIIX), and the Fidelity U.S. Bond Index Fund (FBIDX).

THE FIDELITY FUND PORTFOLIO: 20 YEARS

FSTMX	Actual fund returns 1998–2010 (Wilshire 5000 Index: −0.25% per year) 1991–1997
FSIIX	Actual fund returns 1998–2010 (MSCI EAFE Index: −0.35% per year) 1991–1997
FBIDX	Actual fund returns 1991–2010

THE FIDELITY FUND PORTFOLIO: 10 YEARS

FSTMX	Actual fund returns 2001–2010
FSIIX	Actual fund returns 2001–2010
FBIDX	Actual fund returns 2001–2010

THE FIDELITY FUND PORTFOLIO: 5 YEARS

FSTMX	Actual fund returns 2006–2010
FSIIX	Actual fund returns 2006–2010
FBIDX	Actual fund returns 2006–2010

THE FIDELITY FUND PORTFOLIO: 3 YEARS

FSTMX	Actual fund returns 2008–2010
FSIIX	Actual fund returns 2008–2010
FBIDX	Actual fund returns 2008–2010

T. Rowe Price Funds

The T. Rowe Price Funds you could use to implement the Smartest Index Fund Portfolio are the T. Rowe Price Total Equity Market Fund (POMIX), the T. Rowe Price International Equity Index Fund (PIEQX), and the T. Rowe Price U.S. Bond Index Fund (PBDIX). The following chart shows the allocation of the funds at five risk levels.

Fund	Low Risk	Medium-Low Risk	Medium Risk	Medium-High Risk	High Risk
POMIX	14%	28%	42%	56%	70%
PIEQX	6%	12%	18%	24%	30%
PBDIX	80%	60%	40%	20%	0%

THE T. ROWE PRICE FUND PORTFOLIO: RISK AND RETURN 20 YEARS

ALL PERFORMANCE DATA ARE EXPRESSED IN PERCENT AND ARE HYPOTHETICAL INVESTMENT RESULTS FOR THE PERIOD 1991–2010.

Measure	Low Risk	Medium-Low Risk	Medium Risk	Medium-High Risk	High Risk
Average annual return (geometric)	6.86	7.30	7.59	7.72	7.66
Annualized standard deviation	5.72	8.33	11.61	15.13	18.76
Worst single-calendar-year period	−3.40	−12.25	−21.09	−29.94	−38.78
Worst two-calendar-year period	3.22	−6.15	−15.54	−24.95	−34.37
Worst three-calendar-year period	10.29	−1.28	−15.15	−27.66	−38.90

THE T. ROWE PRICE FUND PORTFOLIO: RISK AND RETURN 10 YEARS

ALL PERFORMANCE DATA ARE EXPRESSED IN PERCENT AND ARE
HYPOTHETICAL INVESTMENT RESULTS FOR THE PERIOD 2001–2010.

Measure	Low Risk	Medium-Low Risk	Medium Risk	Medium-High Risk	High Risk
Average annual return (geometric)	4.66	4.19	3.51	2.58	1.39
Annualized standard deviation	4.15	8.64	13.30	18.00	22.71
Worst single-calendar-year period	−3.40	−12.25	−21.09	−29.94	−38.78
Worst two-calendar-year period	3.22	−6.15	−15.54	−24.95	−34.37
Worst three-calendar-year period	10.29	3.06	−4.74	−13.11	−22.07

THE T. ROWE PRICE FUND PORTFOLIO: RISK AND RETURN 5 YEARS

ALL PERFORMANCE DATA ARE EXPRESSED IN PERCENT AND ARE
HYPOTHETICAL INVESTMENT RESULTS FOR THE PERIOD 2006–2010.

Measure	Low Risk	Medium-Low Risk	Medium Risk	Medium-High Risk	High Risk
Average annual return (geometric)	4.16	3.58	2.75	1.62	0.15
Annualized standard deviation	5.49	10.67	15.89	21.13	26.37
Worst single-calendar-year period	−3.40	−12.25	−21.09	−29.94	−38.78
Worst two-calendar-year period	3.22	−6.15	−15.54	−24.95	−34.37
Worst three-calendar-year period	10.29	3.06	−4.74	-13.11	−22.07

T. ROWE PRICE FUND: RISK AND RETURN 3 YEARS

ALL PERFORMANCE DATA ARE EXPRESSED IN PERCENT AND ARE
HYPOTHETICAL INVESTMENT RESULTS FOR THE PERIOD 2008–2010.

Measure	Low Risk	Medium-Low Risk	Medium Risk	Medium-High Risk	High Risk
Average annual return (geometric)	2.40	0.51	−1.74	−4.39	−7.51
Annualized standard deviation	7.66	14.69	21.72	28.75	35.77
Worst single-calendar-year period	−3.40	−12.25	−21.09	−29.94	−38.78
Worst two-calendar-year period	7.39	1.52	−5.14	−12.60	−20.87
Worst three-calendar-year period	15.93	11.24	5.47	−1.42	−9.46

Raw Data

Raw data used to produce the risk and return data for the T. Rowe
Price Fund Portfolios: T. Rowe Price Total Equity Market Fund
(POMIX), the T. Rowe Price International Equity Index Fund (PIEQX),
and the T. Rowe Price U.S. Bond Index Fund (PBDIX).

THE T. ROWE PRICE FUND PORTFOLIO: 20 YEARS

POMIX	Actual fund returns 1999–2010 (Wilshire 5000 Index: −0.40% per year) 1991–1998
PIEQX	Actual fund returns 2001–2010 (MSCI EAFE Index: −0.50% per year) 1991–2000
PBDIX	Actual fund returns 2001–2010 (Lehman [now Barclays Capital] Aggregate Bond Index: −0.30% per year) 1991–2000

THE T. ROWE PRICE FUND PORTFOLIO: 10 YEARS

POMIX   Actual fund returns 2001–2010

PIEQX   Actual fund returns 2001–2010

PBDIX   Actual fund returns 2001–2010

THE T. ROWE PRICE FUND PORTFOLIO: 5 YEARS

POMIX   Actual fund returns 2006–2010

PIEQX   Actual fund returns 2006–2010

PBDIX   Actual fund returns 2006–2010

THE T. ROWE PRICE FUND PORTFOLIO: 3 YEARS

POMIX   Actual fund returns 2008–2010

PIEQX   Actual fund returns 2008–2010

PBDIX   Actual fund returns 2008–2010

Acknowledgments

I benefited greatly (as I always do) from the insights of John Duff, my publisher and editor at Perigee Books.

My literary agent, Andrea Barzvi, at International Creative Management, has been a continuing source of support and guidance.

I could not have written this book without the assistance of Eddie O'Neal, PhD, a securities expert with Securities Litigation and Consulting Group in Fairfax, Virginia, and Sean Kelly of Kelly & Associates in West Palm Beach, Florida. Their work was limited to structuring the SuperSmart Portfolio and compiling the risk and return data used in this book. All the opinions in the book are mine alone.

It's one thing to write a book and quite another to publicize and distribute it to a wide audience. I am fortunate to have the able assistance of Heather Connor, a publicist at Perigee, and Patrick Nolan and his able sales team. Their help and support has contributed immeasurably to the success of the Smartest series of books.

A special thanks to Mike Solin, who carefully reviewed the entire manuscript and gave me the benefit of his many years of experience and expertise. His insights were invaluable.

And to my wife, Patricia Solin, who patiently edits all my books, including this one: I am fortunate to have her assistance and grateful for her love and support.

Publisher's Note

This publication contains the opinions and ideas of its author. It is intended to provide helpful and informative material on the subject matter covered. It is sold with the understanding that the author and publisher are not engaged in rendering professional services in the book. If the reader requires personal assistance or advice, a competent professional should be consulted. The author and publisher specifically disclaim any responsibility for any liability, loss, or risk, personal or otherwise, which is incurred as a consequence, directly or indirectly, of the use and application of any of the contents of this book.

Trademarks: All terms mentioned in this book that are known to be or are suspected of being trademarks or service marks have been appropriately capitalized. Perigee Books cannot attest to the accuracy of this information. Use of a term in this book should not be regarded as affecting the validity of any trademark or service mark.

Legal disclaimer: This book provides general information that is intended, but not guaranteed, to be correct and up-to-date. The information is not presented as a source of investment, tax, or legal advice. You should not rely on statements or representations made within the book or by any externally referenced sources. If you need investment, tax, or legal advice upon which you intend to rely in the course of your financial, business, or legal affairs, consult a competent, independent financial adviser, accountant, or attorney.

The contents of this book should not be taken as financial advice, or as an offer to buy or sell any securities, fund, type of fund, or financial instruments. It should not be taken as an endorsement or recommendation of any particular company or individual, and no responsibility can be taken for inaccuracies, omissions, or errors. The information presented is not to be considered investment advice. The reader should consult a registered investment adviser or registered dealer prior to making any investment decision.

The author does not assume any responsibility for actions or nonactions taken by people who have read this book, and no one shall be entitled to a claim for detrimental reliance based upon any information provided or expressed herein. Your use of any information provided here does not constitute any type of contractual relationship between yourself and the provider(s) of this information. The author hereby disclaims all responsibility and liability for all use of any information provided in this book.

The materials here are not to be interpreted as establishing an attorney–client or any other relationship between the reader and the author or his firm.

Although great effort has been expended to ensure that only the most meaningful resources are referenced in these pages, the author does not endorse, guarantee, or warranty the accuracy, reliability, or thoroughness of any referenced information, product, or service. Any opinions, advice, statements, services, offers, or other information or content expressed or made available by third parties are those of the author(s) or publisher(s) alone. Reference to other sources of information does not constitute a referral, endorsement, or recommendation of any product or service. The existence of any particular reference is simply intended to imply potential interest to the reader.

The views expressed herein are exclusively those of the author and do not represent the views of any other person or any organization with which the author is, or may be, associated.

Index

Page number in **bold** indicate tables.